AMERICAN PRIMITIVE

AMERICAN

Discoveries in Folk Sculpture

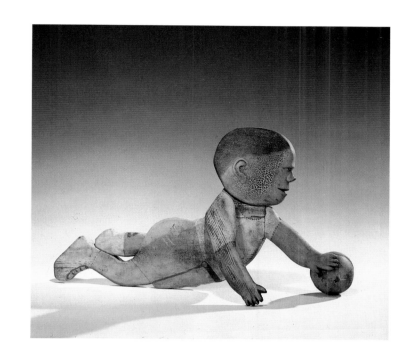

PRIMITIVE

ROGER RICCO · FRANK MARESCA

WITH JULIA WEISSMAN
PHOTOGRAPHS BY FRANK MARESCA
AND EDWARD SHOFFSTALL

ALFRED A. KNOPF

NEW YORK   1988

THIS IS A BORZOI BOOK
PUBLISHED BY ALFRED A. KNOPF, INC.

LIBRARY OF CONGRESS
CATALOGING-IN-PUBLICATION DATA

Ricco, Roger.
    American primitive.

    Bibliography: p.
    1. Folk art—United States.   2. Sculpture,
American.   3. Primitivism in art—United States.
I. Maresca, Frank.   II. Weissman, Julia.
III. Title.
NK805.R53   1988   730'.0973   88-45341
ISBN 0-394-54467-6

Manufactured in Italy
First Edition

Contents

Acknowledgments

THIS BOOK could not have come into being without the enthusiastic generosity of the individuals and galleries whose art appears here and who contributed so willingly to its contents, both materially and ideologically.

Thanks, too, are owed to: Mary Ann Demos for her valuable research on the Woodbridge figures; Mary Ann Sievert, Lex Boterf and Carl Bellavia for their cheerful assistance in the arduous task of collating captions and photographs.

To Alice Quinn and Vicky Wilson, our editors, special gratitude for their unwavering interest and support, guidance and unfailing patience; and to Peter Andersen, who designed a beautiful book.

We would like to acknowledge a special indebtedness to James Kronen, whose unique vision and excitement for this material inspired us and many of the collectors whose objects appear in this book.

And finally, we owe special thanks to Elizabeth Johnson, our good friend and inspirational collaborator, without whom there would have been no book.

Foreword

THIS BOOK documents a body of American art about which there has been and still is uncertainty and even disagreement, not only about its nomenclature but also about where it belongs in the hierarchy of American art. Conventional art history, not finding a comfortable place for it, has shied away from taking it seriously.

Some of it is by known artists, much of it is anonymous, some is marvelously elegant in design, line and form, and some is raw and desperate, often fetishlike in power. We are not the first to have been moved by the force of this art and there have been books prior to this one, but what we have found as collectors as well as dealers is that there is a vast amount of it—fresh and audacious, with a special quality of unselfconsciousness of approach—that has never been exhibited in a show or museum or illustrated anywhere: wonderful things, macabre, visionary, offbeat, splendid and plain beautiful.

The pieces in this book were made by people with no formal training in art. They are expressive, in our minds, of a need that exists in the most ordinary of humans to put a vision into a form that has more physical substance than words, and thus declare, "I exist and I am an individual."

These are images made by people with a personal need to create, to say something with art, and more often than not, with neither the hope nor the intention that their works would be acknowledged as art or they as artists.

What we responded to in each case was the underlying independence of the sensibility that produced the work, the clarity of vision, a quality of perplexity and mystery, of freshness of form and a surprising resolution that sets all the pieces apart from the common and brings them together, distinctly establishing a category of art separate from those pieces, however magnificent—factory weathervanes, quilts, samplers and the like—that emerged from a craft tradition.

The artists are from all walks of life and a wide variety of socio-economic and ethnic backgrounds. Many were elderly when they found themselves unable to resist a pressing urge to create. Several among them have said they were told by God to make art, or had received instructions from a vision to cut stone or carve wood. Others almost wandered into making art, and there found serenity, even sanity, making what they saw inside their heads. Still others were simply provincial craftsmen who found it necessary to make something, a decoy, for example, or a lampstand, because it pertained to their trade or business.

In sum, these are newly discovered or previously unpublished works by untutored artists with personal, often eccentric visions and concepts.

Our enthusiasm for this art found its counterpart among a special group of collectors who were, not unlike the artists themselves, individualistic, even idiosyncratic, in their taste and their pursuit. They search, they buy, they collect with a single-minded faith in its validity and distinction as American fine art. Our book, then, is a tribute to those people whose special visions and ingenuity made them into artists though they were unaware of it, and to those collectors who recognized the art and took it to their hearts.

ROGER RICCO / FRANK MARESCA

AMERICAN PRIMITIVE

INTRODUCTION

IN THE ANNALS of American art, there are not very many comprehensive surveys of American sculpture. Moreover, in such histories as are available, short shrift is given to sculpture by backwater or sidestream (to differentiate them from mainstream) artists, who are more or less isolated under the moot rubric of folk art, or as primitive, "outsider," visionary and, more recently, alienated. Most art historians, if they take note of it at all, tend to deal with it rather summarily. They seem to regard it as an aesthetically interesting, even valid, but nonetheless passing phase in American art history rather than a perseveringly cogent art phenomenon with as much saliency as any other sculptural expression in the general continuum of American art.

Even Wayne Craven, a noted American art historian, though he pays tribute to early American carvers in *Sculpture in America*,[1] seems to have turned a blind eye to later sculpture or carving done by nonprofessionals outside shops or studios. It is almost as if work by untrained sculptors after the first quarter of the nineteenth century was simply nonexistent or, if not done by trade or profession, not worthy of discussion. Or it may be that his taste, like that of John Manfredi, a sociologist who writes about art, "runs to products of the studio, the conservatory and ivory towers."[2]

Yet sculpture of quality not only has been but continues to be produced outside those realms. That the works of untaught artists are in the form of objects such as decoys, weathervanes, whirligigs, canes, icons, toys or lampstands does not make them any less viable as works of art than the primitive and naive sculptures of other societies.

American artists who have been in the forefront of altering trends in art since the turn of the century have appreciated this. Robert Goldwater, in his now classic book *Primitivism and Modern Art,*[3] wrote of the effect of primitive sculpture of nonindustrial societies on the European artists who were then rejecting academism. A similar ferment was occurring in the United States among avant-garde American artists who had gone to France to study and had returned. They were, in a sense, mutineers, rebelling against not only academism and naturalism but even impressionism. Taking a cue from their European counterparts and former mentors, they looked first for inspiration in American aboriginal art and began to study the limited public collections of what came to be called American folk art, which heretofore was valued more as a curiosity or for its relationship to local history than for its place in American art history.

The Whitney Studio Club, precursor to the present Whitney Museum of American Art, was among the first to exhibit publicly this intriguing art, in 1924. Shows followed at the Dudensing Gallery in New York, at the Nadelman Museum of Folk Art in Riverdale, New York (sculptor Eli Nadelman's style frankly derived from American naive sculpture, although he was a modernist), and at Isabel Carleton Wilde's Gallery in Cambridge, Massachusetts.

The first major public institution to stage an exhibition devoted exclusively to outstanding American sculpture by untrained artists was the Newark Museum in New Jersey. It was organized in 1931 by Holger Cahill, who, together with Edith Halpert Gregory, mounted the show "American Folk Art: The Art of the Common Man in America, 1750–1900" at the Museum of Modern Art in New York City, in 1932.

The sculpture in that show related almost entirely to everyday life, and most of the works had been conceived for daily use: they were examples of how need and purpose served as accidental or incidental stimuli for artistic expression. But the show was also important because the works were

Uncle Sam. Anonymous. Wood with polychrome. This 19th-century Uncle Sam wears a tin collar and holds a glass milk bottle in his hand, suggesting that it was a trade figure. H: 26¹/₂". (Private Collection)

exhibited as *art,* not artifacts, in a museum dedicated to modern art, and were so exhibited with a perceived affinity to the development of modernism in American art. It's been said that those American artists who collected indigenous primitive and naive art did so "in search of their historical American roots, and thus served as a reply to critics who complained that American modern art was only another version of decadent European civilization."[4] Maybe, but it is equally likely that what intrigued those early artist-collectors was not merely the historical significance or antiquity of the works but their often startling audacity of form or style, and a sort of *reductio ad veritas,* a refreshing reminder of the innocent origins of art within the individual. They had, William Zorach wrote, "an amazing simplicity of effort and intention."[5] Such works excited American artists with a bent for artistic heresy in much the same way that the art of primitive peoples excited European artists. It is that same eclectic "otherness" in latter-day American naive and primitive artists that has attracted mainstream artists of our own time.

The 1900 cut-off date for the 1932 exhibition at the Museum of Modern Art was selected, evidently, in the belief that the swift rise of industrialism, mass media, photography, communications, and even rapid transit had caused a near-total dissolution of handcraft as a necessary domestic occupation and therefore the demise of art created by folk. Not so. Though social circumstance and the nature of the incentive may have changed, the urge to create has by no means been bred out of the bone of the "common people." They are as productive and as naively original as untaught artists were in the years prior to the machine and electronic ages.

It was perhaps unfortunate, too, that the 1932 exhibit carried the title "American Folk Art," for want, as Cahill acknowledged, of a more exact descriptive definition of the works. Admittedly, American primitive and naive sculpture differs from that of the peoples of nonindustrial societies. American works, exclusive of American Indian and New Mexico Santeros, do not have an ethnological element that unifies them as belonging to a particular group. They are not, except in rare cases like the Woodbridge figures on p. 35, motivated by ritualistic ideology indigenous to one group or community. But calling the work folk art may have somewhat obscured the significance of the exhibition's being held in the Museum of Modern Art: by situating American primitive and naive art in the company of modern art, it was effectively removed from the parochialism of "folk art."

Though MOMA more or less put the imprimatur of "art" on objects made by the American "common man," the American public—which has learned to appreciate African and other primitive sculpture—has been slow to accept its own folk art as fine art. It has been something of an underground movement in the art world, but a nonetheless persistent one, that surfaced in 1962 with the establishment of the Museum of Early American Folk Art.

As the name indicated, the founders had a conservative attitude about what should be in the museum. However, one of the board members with a less doctrinaire approach, Herbert W. Hemphill, Jr., who also functioned as curator, began to discover not only in his activities as a collector but in his curatorial searches that he was being attracted to works done after 1900 and, indeed, that striking "folk" art was still being produced by living "folk" artists. Largely as a result of his persuasion, the museum changed its name and became simply the Museum of American Folk Art. In 1970, under Hemphill's curatorship, the museum held its first exhibition devoted entirely to twentieth-century works.

Among the first to pick up on this lead was Michael Hall, a contemporary constructionist sculptor and teacher at the prestigious Cranbrook Academy in Michigan. Hall mounted an exhibition at the Cranbrook Academy Art Galleries in November 1971 called "American Folk Sculpture: The Personal and the Eccentric." There is a hint of dissatisfaction with the designation "folk art" in Hall's introduction to the catalogue for his exhibition, for he speaks of "what has been called 'American Folk Art,'" suggesting that it was called so only because the artists, "unlike generally without a profit motive . . . farmers, tradesmen, barbers, or vagabonds who at some moment in their lives responded to the urge to 'make something.'"[6]

This dissatisfaction is echoed in an essay by Daniel Robbins in the catalogue for a show held at the Brooklyn Museum in 1976, "Folk Sculpture, USA," curated by Hemphill.[7] Robbins not only questioned the concept of "folk" with reference to the sculpture in the show but also balked at the lack of scholarly research that might have determined if it really was "folk"—that is, art rooted in a community tradition and based on transmitted design and use—or whether it was naive work inspired and influenced, as was the naive art of Europe, by sophisticated work on public display or in the print medium.

Pipe bowl. Anonymous. Maple. Found in Ohio. Late 19th century. L: 5″; H: 3″; w: 2″. (Collection of Timothy and Pamela Hill)

It is quite true that American "folk" sculpture has, more than painting, eluded scholarly research along the lines Robbins suggested; however, the pursuit of the necessary provenance is apt to become something of an exercise in frustration. Painting—portraiture and genre—is and has generally been accepted as "art" to be displayed and treasured as such, which means that works often remained in the family and did not wander too far afield. Therefore there might be extant some record of them as to date and area, and even first cost. American folk or naive painters usually produced bodies of works, so it has been possible, even in the absence of signatures, to study output and survey the publications and reproductions of their periods to see how and how much folk painters emulated the European and American trained painters of the period—or deviated from them.

Sculpture is another matter altogether. Since so few works were created as art per se, they were not always cherished, but instead were exiled to storerooms, barns, trunks, jumble sales, flea markets and junk shops. Their survival, as in the case of many of the limberjacks and the whirligigs illustrated in this book, has been a matter of chance—that chance, frequently, being the discerning eye of a collector, art dealer or artist. But in all too many instances, the buyer's instinct for art has been sharper than his or her curiosity about a work's provenance; consequently, while it might be possible to make an assumption about the approximate date of a work, there is often not much information recorded about its origin before the last point of purchase, and it is rare that any information at all about the artist turns up.

Some of the difficulties inherent in attempting the kind of research Robbins considers necessary are elucidated by Lynette I. Rhodes in her particularly thoughtful and thought-provoking introduction to the catalogue for the Cleveland Museum of Art's 1978 exhibition "American Folk Art: From the Traditional to the Naive." Part of the problem is the term "folk art." Rhodes says, "It must be remembered that the folk arts are related to the daily material and spiritual needs of ordinary peoples . . . in many cultures . . . and are expressions of the masses, reflecting the direction of their daily life."[8] Here she makes a statement that underlines the character of *this* art, what it is that makes it both American and distinctive: "The American emphasis on individuality is unique among world folk art, making it more appropriately naive rather than folk."[9]

It is not that there is no tradition at all underlying American folk or naive sculpture. In a manner of speaking, it can be (and has been) said to have come out of a handcraft tradition, but it is a tradition of crafting—that is, making—but not dictated by shop or studio training. There is, consequently, a general absence of traditionally determined style or technique. These works are strikingly individualistic, the early as well as the contemporary, unique because of the manner in which a tradition has been recollected, as in canes evocative of African sculpture, or in a religious carving, or how an event purveyed through the artist's vision becomes a unique interpretation. The busts of Seward and Admiral Dewey (pp. 77, 78) were evidently expressions of admiration prompted by reports of their exploits in the newspapers of the time; the maker of the "Great White Hope" windup toy (p. 145) felt stirred by media accounts of a boxing match that was more than just a sports event, but had racial significance.

Robbins objected to classifying the art according to "object-type," and we do not necessarily disagree with that view. Nonetheless, we felt it appropriate to allocate the works presented here in categories that seemed to reflect the intention of their makers, those intentions being, in many instances, use of one kind or another. It is almost a given in primitive or naive sculpture up until very recent years that works were not necessarily simply or solely to be enjoyed or experienced aesthetically. But, as Erwin Panofsky avers, a work of art "always has aesthetic significance . . . whether or not it serves some practical purpose.[10] The importance of these works lies in their aesthetic significance: each one was selected for having an aspect of the artist's unique, personal vision of his or her subject, whether the artist intended the piece to be used for something other than art alone or whether it was made to be art, as many of the works in Chapter 10 were, for all that the artists may not have had any ambition to be regarded as artists.

In the latter group, many of the works have surprising similarities to certain modern expressionist or primitivistic sculpture. In some cases, as in Stanley Papio's, the work presents the problem of defining what makes an artist naive or primitive. The sophistication of Papio's assemblage rivals that of mainstream metalist sculptors who, like Papio, used or incorporated industrial refuse in their sculptures. However, Papio, though a skilled welder, was totally untrained as an artist, and if his work seems sophisticated it is due not so much to his awareness of sculptural art as it probably is to the sophistication of the found automobile parts he used. It seems fair

Miniature bird. H: 4¹/₂″; L: 5¹/₂″. (Collection of Patricia Guthman)

to call an artist like Papio a genius, perhaps a *naive-savant,* for his intuitive ability to disassociate the shapes of objects from their original use or context and to assemble those shapes into another, distinctive form that merits, as much as any other kind of sculpture, being called fine art.

To borrow a remark by Mark Stevens in *Newsweek* of August 22, 1977, "the trick in looking at good naive art is to savor the sophistication and the naiveté together."

These works—call them naive, call them primitive—are to be savored as art.

JULIA WEISSMAN

1

FIGURATIVE

EVER SINCE the first drawings were sketched on Ice Age cave walls and the female figure apotheosized in the heavily bosomed little stone Venus of Willendorf, no subject, until the onset of nonobjective art, has preoccupied artists more than the human figure. Using any material that would make a mark or put a color on a flat surface, or by shaping mud and molding clay, bending or casting metal, chipping wood, bone, ivory and stone, artists have transmogrified gods and angels, devils and evil spirits into human form. Artists have idealized or satirized royalty, nobleman and commoner alike, shown them in every position possible (and some not)—prone, sitting, kneeling and standing—in every activity from battling to dancing, in every mood from sad or prayerful to angry or ecstatic, as saint or sinner, as virtue or eroticism personified.

In its earliest manifestations in the history of art, the human figure, whether sketched, painted or sculpted, was a basic representation with elementary identifying details, classic examples being the ancient Cycladic sculptures and early Egyptian painted drawings on tomb walls. As civilizations became more complex, the services to which art was put broadened, and artists became more and more capable of, as well as interested in,

FIG. 1. *Baby in a chair.* Anonymous. Wood with polychrome. Found in upstate New York. Carved from a single piece of wood. Late 19th century. H: 12¹/₄″. (Private Collection)

realistically rendering human anatomy in both painting and sculpting. However, the techniques of each art method are quite different.

Painting became in effect an art of deception, offering an illusion of three-dimensional corporeality placed in space, depth and light seemingly defined as the eyes define them. The actual light in which or under which a painting is seen rarely alters its aspect, effect or meaning.

Sculpture, on the other hand, is "real": it requires and exists in real space, just as we do, for it has volume as well as shape. Moreover, its appearance, its effect and even its meaning can change as the light in or under which it is placed changes.

While the ability to render an entity with exactness is a goal many trained artists strive for, nonetheless a subject can be and often is dynamically and creatively expressed in spite of—or perhaps even because of— the absence of such skill. Far more important than doctrinaire techniques is a quality often evident in primitive and naive art, not only of previous eras but in the present: an intuitive ability to distill an idea about a subject and make a direct and basic statement. The absence of sophisticated art "knowledge" makes the self-taught artist unafraid of using whatever material is available and using whatever tools are at hand to depict any subject in mind in any way that the artist finds feasible for "getting it down." Naives and primitives have no qualms about breaking rules they are, in any case, unaware of, no fears that their methods won't work, and, since it is not their major concern, no worries that their work will not sell. Such innocent defiance results in daring solutions and bold art.

And therein lies the difference between the naive and the amateur, who is often also a self-taught artist. Amateurs aspire to imitate academic art; they have learned, even educated, concepts of art and produce art based on an outer imposition of what art should be. The naive artist of authentic talent has a truly independent vision. If, for example, the subject of a child or infant, such as Fig. 1 or Fig. 31, had been attempted by an amateur rather than a gifted naive, the image would very likely have been a conventional one. Instead, the child in the chair has an electric vitality and character of unpredictable potential. As for Fig. 31, because of the odd interplay between the flat cutout figure and the fully rounded ball, one is infected with a sense of unease rather than benignancy.

Subtlety is rarely a naive's forte. Where the trained artist will handle a subject like sexuality with suggestive finesse, the naive is more apt to be

FIG. 2. *Scarecrow.* Anonymous. Wood, tree branches, wire, traces of paint. Found in Pennsylvania. Only the head and the neck of this figure were carved; the arms and legs are fallen branches, the torso fashioned out of flexible slats from a fruit crate and the whole held together with fence wire. Ca. 1930–40. H: 94″; W: 18″. (Private Collection)

FIG. 3. *Bust of a woman* by Stanley Papio. Welded assemblage of chromed-steel automobile bumpers. Ca. 1959. H: 25″. (Private Collection)

STANLEY PAPIO, Canadian-born (1915–82), spent most of his adult life in Key Largo, Florida, after serving a stint in the American Navy, where he learned welding. Settling in an undeveloped area of Key Largo, he bought a lot, which he filled with junk appropriate to his trade: car parts and metal objects of every sort from plumbing pipes to bedsprings. When latecomers to the area took him to court for creating an eyesore, his irritation led him to start welding his "junk" into sculpture that lampooned his neighbors and their "kangaroo court." He gave his figures names such as "Two-faced Woman," "Greedy Grit the Contractor" (a satire on the developers desecrating the Florida Keys' natural charm), "Mary the Good Girl." Told by tourists that he was a folk artist, he called his assembly of figures his Folk Art Museum, and charged visitors 25¢ admission.

overt and forthright. Nonetheless, though the facial expression of the full-figured logging-camp woman (Fig. 10) is serene, the exaggerated voluptuousness of her figure is universally clear in meaning. This is true as well of the erotic male figure, Fig. 47, whose explicit gesture conveys an unmistakable message but whose expression is almost detached from the action of the body.

The uses of the human figure in naive and primitive art are, as in all cultures and on all levels of art, varied. As servant, it can, like the telamon (Fig. 52), hold up a platform and so become a stand for a lamp or vase; or stand on a tradesman's counter, as did the tobacconist figure, presenting a box once filled with cigars (Fig. 24).

Then there are those figures that the naive or primitive artist sees lurking in natural shapes or found objects. Shiny automobile parts, welded

FIG. 4. (BELOW) *Gatepost figure* by Joe Mullet. Stone. The twin of this primitive figure bears a plate on its breast with the inscription "carved by Joe Mullet." It is believed to have been made early in the 20th century. H: 26″; W: 11¼″; D: 7½″. (Collection of Richard Levey and Sigrid Christiansen)

FIG. 5. (ABOVE) *Female figure* by Raymond Coins. Stone. Coins, now in his eighties, began carving over twenty years ago. Learning that Indian arrowheads found on his farm in North Carolina were worth money, he began making replicas of them, and then, inspired by the shapes of the stones, boulders, tree roots and fallen branches in his fields, he began carving anthropomorphic figures and animals. This figure bears a striking similarity to Eskimo stone sculpture, though Coins has said that he carves what he sees in his dreams. Ca. 1980. H: 23½″; W: 17″. (Courtesy Robert N. Hicklin, Jr.)

together by Stanley Papio, become human figures (Fig. 3); a root yielded a Janus-faced man (Fig. 46), and a formidable scarecrow (Fig. 2) was assembled from found wood pieces and natural tree forms. Other figures were apparently meant to be personal portraits (Figs. 9 and 21), but still others seem to be wholly idiosyncratic, their inspiration and purpose elusive.

FIG. 6. (LEFT) *Angel* by Raymond Coins. Stone. Inscribed at the base: "In God We Trust." Signed on the reverse. Ca. 1970–80. H: 35″; W: 28″; D: 5½″. (Private Collection)

FIGS. 7, 8. (OPPOSITE) Bathing beauty lampstands. Anonymous. Maple, pine and walnut with polychrome. These were used in an Atlantic City hotel lobby to symbolize the resort's charms. Ca. 1925. H: 46″. (7. Collection of Timothy and Pamela Hill; 8. Brian Collection)

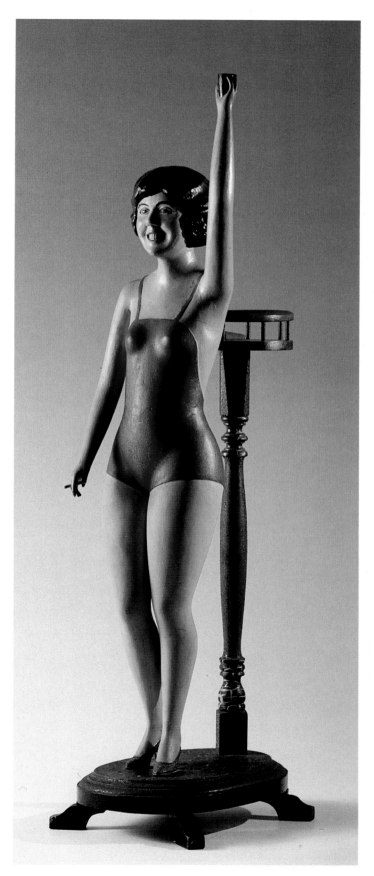

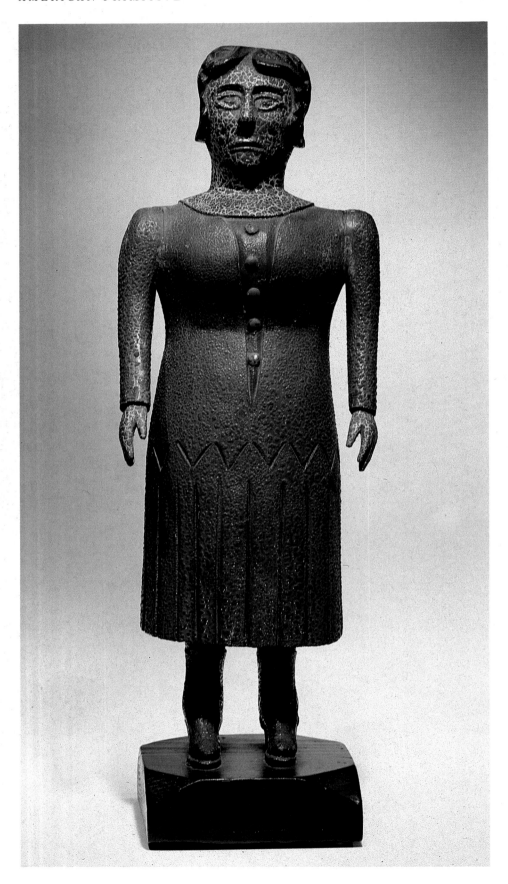

FIG. 9. (LEFT) *Figure of a woman.* Anonymous. Wood with polychrome. Her dress seems to date this sturdy, stern-visaged woman at around 1920. The crackling of the paint has become an integral part of the aesthetic force of this figure. H: 19″. (Collection of Isobel and Harvey Kahn)

FIG. 10. (OPPOSITE) *Female figure.* Anonymous. Pine with polychrome. Found in a logging camp in Maine, this figure had been placed in front of a bunkhouse, presumably by its maker. For all its function as a "pinup," the sculpture has a poignantly wistful as well as gently erotic quality. Early 20th century. H: 51″. (Private Collection)

FIG. 11. *Venus.* Anonymous. Wood, red stain, varnish, brass nipples. Dubbed "Venus" because it is armless, this figure evokes budding adolescence. It was found in the South. Ca. 1920–30. H: 18½". (Blumert-Fiore Collection)

FIG. 12. (BELOW) *Penholder*. Anonymous. Hammered steel skirt, copper head, aluminum paint, lead weight. Found in southern New England, probably a paperweight as well as a penholder. Ca. 1930–40. H: 13″. (The Hall Collection of American Folk and Isolate Art)

FIG. 13. (CENTER) *Female figure*. Anonymous. Walnut. Found in Ohio. Late 19th century. H: 16″; base: W: 6½″; D: 7″. (Collection of Timothy and Pamela Hill)

FIG. 14. (RIGHT) *Figure of a woman*. Anonymous. Wood. Found in Florida. The stance and the fact that its open mouth is deeply carved suggests this figure is singing. Ca. 1870–90. H: 11″. (Private Collection)

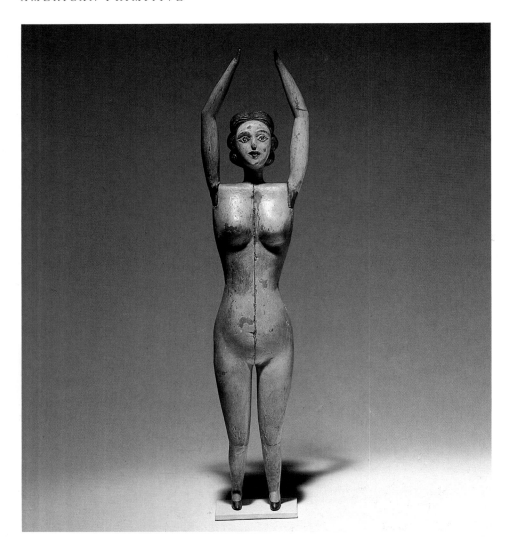

FIG. 15. (LEFT) *Woman with raised arms.* Anonymous. Maple with polychrome. Found in Wisconsin. Ca. 1925. H: 21″. (Collection of Timothy and Pamela Hill)

FIG. 16. (BELOW) *Reclining nude.* Anonymous. Wood with polychrome. This carving once hung in a bar in San Francisco. First quarter 20th century. H: 14″; L: 34½″; D: 4″. (Marvel Collection)

FIG. 17. (OPPOSITE) *Display mannequin.* Anonymous. Wood with polychrome. Although evidently used for display purposes, this carving is at the same time very personal and erotic. Found in the Midwest. Ca. 1940s. Life-sized. (Private Collection)

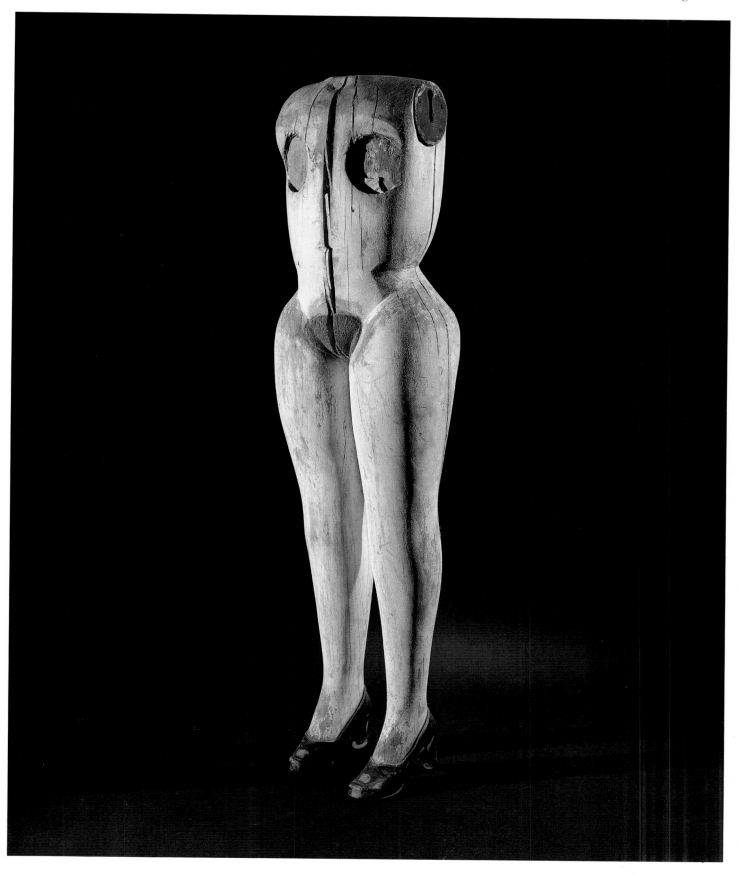

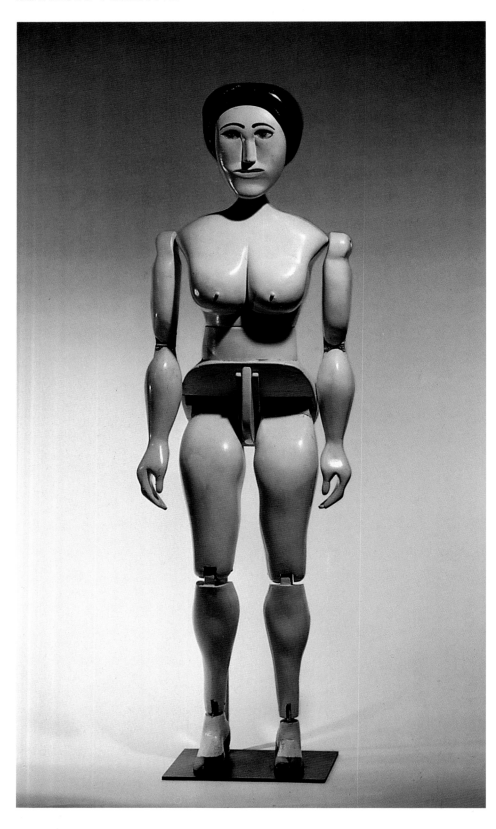

FIG. 18. (LEFT) *Jointed mannequin.* Anonymous. Wood with polychrome. The relatively small size of this figure precludes its use as a traditional mannequin. It probably was clothed, but its function is unknown. Ca. 1930–40. H: 49½". (Private Collection)

FIG. 19. (BELOW) *Tobacconist's counter figure.* Anonymous. Wood, traces of blue paint. Carved out of one piece of wood, except for the drawer in the box, which was made from a cigar box, evidently used for matches and inscribed "Nathan humphrey" (*sic*). Late 19th century. H: 32"; W: 7"; D: 7¾". (Didi and David Barrett Collection)

FIG. 20. (RIGHT) *Janus figures.* Anonymous. Soapstone, with dark patina. Found in a home in Lumpkin County, Georgia. Late 18th, early 19th century. H: 4″; front: w: 3″; side: w: 6″. (Collection of George Meyer)

FIG. 21. (BELOW LEFT) *Seated lady* by Taylor Johnson. Wood with polychrome. Johnson lived in Crisfield, Maryland. Ca. 1925. H: 9″; w: 6″; D: 4″. (Courtesy Timothy and Pamela Hill)

FIG. 22. (BELOW RIGHT) *Standing female figure.* Anonymous. Wood with polychrome. Found in Kentucky. Local lore suggests it was made as a companion for a child. It stood exposed on a porch. Ca. 1910. H: 56″; w: 12¹/₂″; D: 6″. (Private Collection)

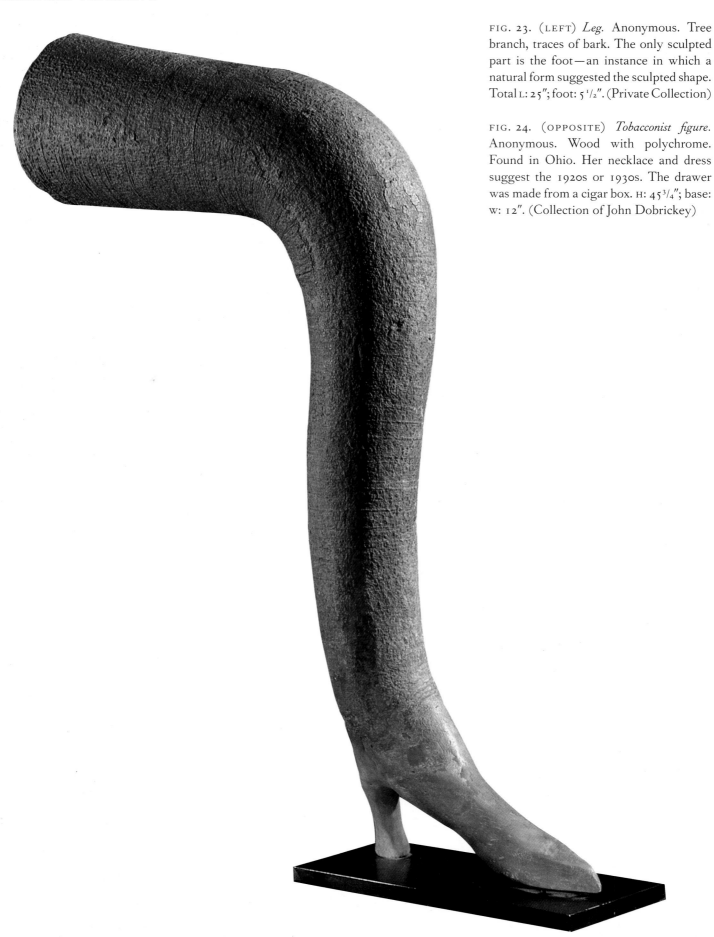

FIG. 23. (LEFT) *Leg.* Anonymous. Tree branch, traces of bark. The only sculpted part is the foot—an instance in which a natural form suggested the sculpted shape. Total L: 25″; foot: 5 ½″. (Private Collection)

FIG. 24. (OPPOSITE) *Tobacconist figure.* Anonymous. Wood with polychrome. Found in Ohio. Her necklace and dress suggest the 1920s or 1930s. The drawer was made from a cigar box. H: 45 ¾″; base: w: 12″. (Collection of John Dobrickey)

FIG. 25. (OPPOSITE) *Dancing figure*. Anonymous. Wood and polychrome. Portrayal of such exuberant motion is rare in American naive sculpture. Ca. 1920–30. H: 11″. (Private Collection)

FIG. 26. (ABOVE) *Dancing figure*. Anonymous. Wood, black paint, articulated arms. This figure is rare in that it cannot stand without support, yet in every position that it is placed, it conveys a wonderful vitality of movement. Late 1930s. H: 4″. (Private Collection)

FIG. 27. (RIGHT) *Rubber figure*. Anonymous. Raw rubber, rubber sheeting. Probably an after-work piece created as a toy or doll by a worker in a rubber plant. 20th century. H: 9″. (Private Collection)

FIG. 28. (FAR RIGHT) *Figurative pencil box* by Stephen Polaha. Wood, stain, varnish, metal hinges. The artist, who lived in Pennsylvania and died around 1960, could have been influenced by the King Tut rage of the early 1920s, when the tomb was first uncovered. Mid-20th century. L: 11″; D: 3¹/₂″; W: 3″. (Private Collection)

FIG. 29. (OPPOSITE) *Pair of dolls* by Isabelle Greathouse (1856–1938), Butler City, Kentucky. Woman and man. Coconut head, cloth polychrome. Ca. 1880–90. Man: H: 23″; W: 7″; D: 3¹/₂″. Woman: H: 13″; W: 5″; D: 3″. (Private Collection)

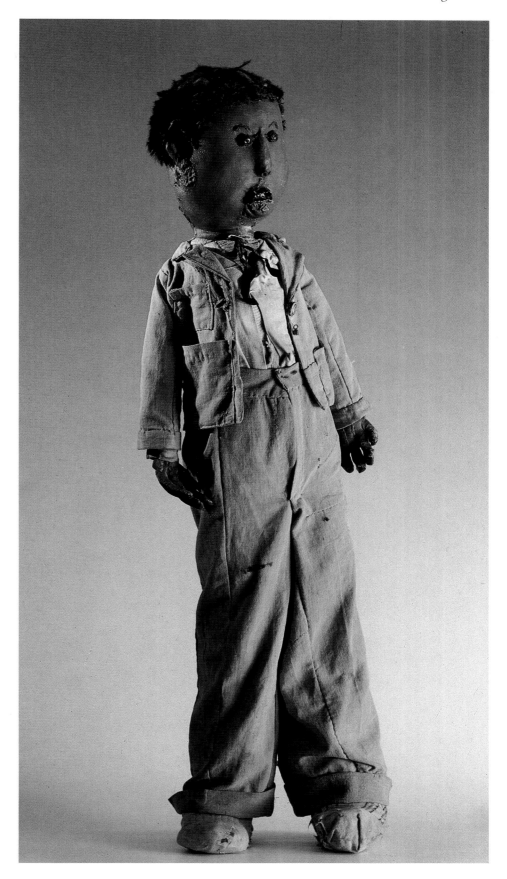

FIG. 30. (RIGHT) *Doll.* Anonymous. Painted canvas, fabric, button eyes, fur hair, crocheted lips and hands. The fingernails and teeth are probably made from dog's teeth. Found in Alabama, this doll bears a similarity to Bembe (African) funeral figures. Early 20th century. H: 38″. (The Hall Collection of American Folk and Isolate Art)

FIG. 31. (OPPOSITE) *Baby with ball sign.* Anonymous. Wood with polychrome. From an orphanage in Millbrook, New York, where it was affixed to the front gate. The body is flat, the ball is round. Mid-20th century. L: 27″; H: 15″. (Private Collection)

FIG. 32. (RIGHT) *"Beggar" figures.* Anonymous. Wood, fabric, leather shoes. Found in South Carolina. Their purpose is unknown. Ca. 1860–70. H, seated: 36″. (Private Collection)

FIG. 33. (BELOW) *Female figure.* Anonymous. Wood with polychrome. Origin unknown. A rare example in naive sculpture of a figure in motion, perhaps dancing or running. Ca. 1920–30. H: 17″. (Private Collection)

FIG. 34. (BELOW RIGHT) *Erotic figures in coffin boxes.* Anonymous. Pine. The boxes encasing these figures have lids. Judging from the aged appearance of the wood, they probably date from the late 19th or early 20th century. H: 7¹/₂″; W: 2³/₄″; D: 1³/₄″. (Collection of Isobel and Harvey Kahn).

FIG. 35. (LEFT AND OPPOSITE) *The Wood-bridge figures.* Anonymous. Wood, poly-chromed. More than a hundred such figures ranging in size from 4^1/$_2$″ to 7^3/$_4$″ high, found ca. 1950 in a shed in Woodbridge, New Jersey. Virtually every figure has a hole in the top of the head fitted with a plug carved in the shape of a penis. The shed was known to be a gathering place or chapel as late as the 1940s, and the figures were presumably ritual fertility fetishes. (Private Collection)

FIG. 36. (FAR LEFT) *Brush man, trade stim-ulator.* Anonymous. This life-sized figure, found in the Midwest, once had light bulbs for eyes. It is assumed to have been made by a shopkeeper as a catchy display for his wares. Ca. 1930–40. H: 70″; W: 26″; D: 16″. (Courtesy Alan Stone Gallery, New York City)

FIG. 37. (LEFT) *Butler.* Anonymous. Wood with polychrome. Although a common type of ashtray holder, this one is unusually individualized and sculptural. Its face is fully carved, its buttons are of brass. Ca. 1920–30. H: 34″. (Collection of Michael and Elizabeth Friedman)

FIG. 38. (BELOW) *Cigar store Indian.* Anonymous. Wood with polychrome. Found in Pennsylvania, this figure is powerful in its simplicity. The tonsure (in-stead of the more common feathered head-dress) indicates it may have been intended to represent a Mohawk. Early 20th century. H: 66″; W: 18″. (Courtesy Harris Diamant Gallery, New York City)

FIG. 39. (ABOVE) *Pair of figures* by Herman Bridgers. Wood with white paint, tar. Ca. 1979. H: 28″; W: 21″; D: 16¹/₂″. (Collection of Robert Lynch)

FIG. 40. (RIGHT) *Pair of figures* by Herman Bridgers. Wood with off-white paint, tar. Ca. 1978. H: 36″; W: 24″; D: 14″. (Collection of Robert Lynch)

HERMAN BRIDGERS was born in 1913, in North Carolina. A retired ditchdigger, Bridgers still digs graves for pocket change. His first figures were cut to post around a rural church he had built, in order to distinguish it from another very close by.

FIG. 41. (FAR LEFT) *Skeleton* by Phillip Pellegrino. Leather. The artist, now in his sixties, is a retired shoemaker. This is but one of numerous figures he has made out of pieces of leftover leather. Ca. 1950. H: 12″. (Private Collection)

FIG. 42. (LEFT) *Preacher.* Anonymous. Ox vertebra, polychrome. This figure was found in Pennsylvania, though similar ones have been found in upstate New York. The maker of this one saw the inherent shape in the form of the bone. Late 19th century. H: 4³/₄″; W: 3″; D: 3¹/₂″. (Collection of Cynthia Beneduce)

FIG. 43. (BELOW) *Preacher.* Anonymous. Wood with polychrome, nails and string. Found in Pennsylvania. Late 19th, early 20th century. H: 12″. (Private Collection)

FIG. 44. (OPPOSITE) *Scarecrow.* Anonymous. Baseball bats, metal bucket, thermos bottle, oil spout and other found objects. Found in the Midwest, this scarecrow seems to depict a bandit. Ca. 1920–40. H: 59″. (Carl Hammer Gallery; photograph Cheri Eisenberg)

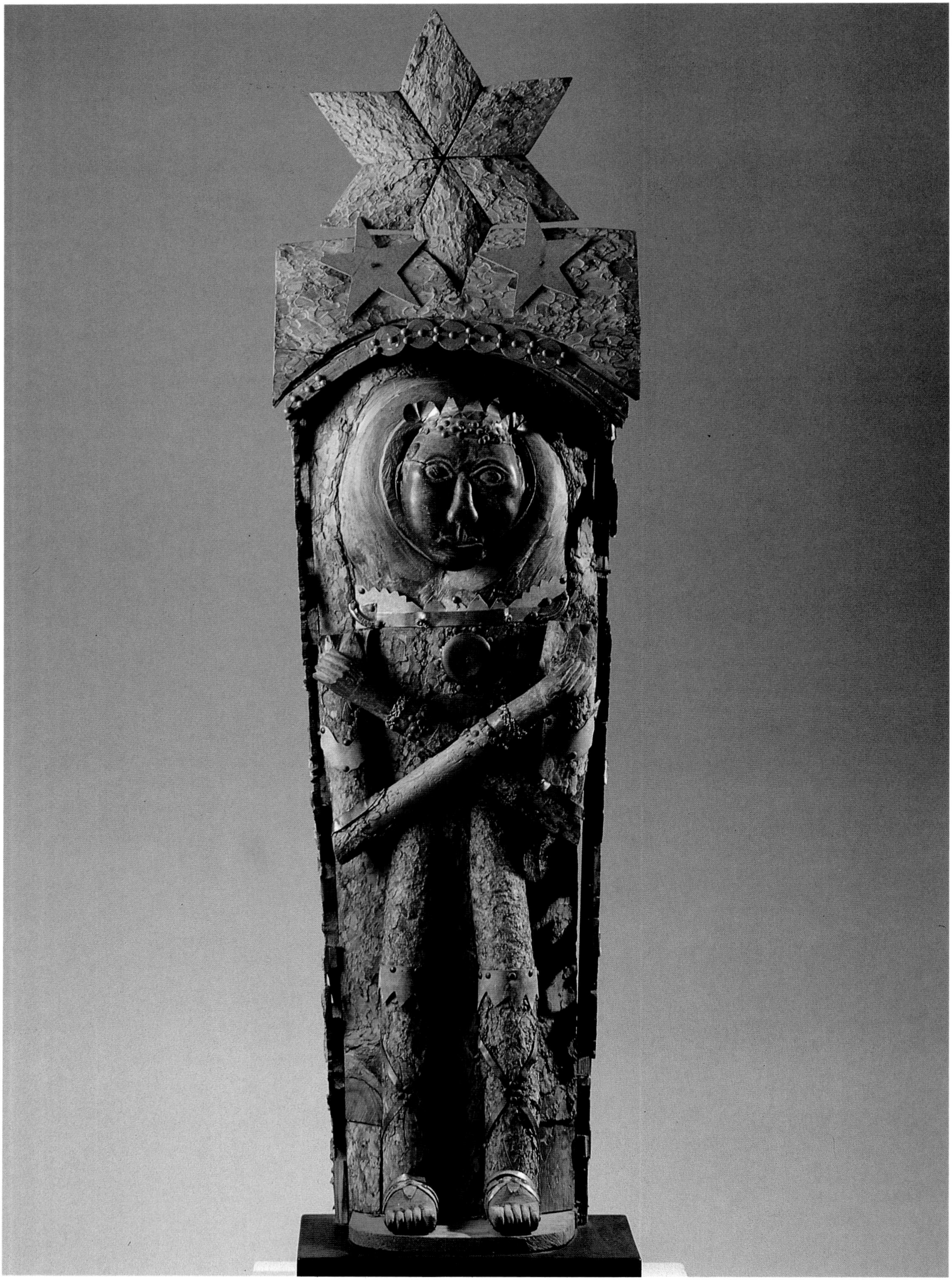

FIG. 45. (OPPOSITE) *Iconic figure* by Thomas Carlton. Tree branches and trunk, root, wood, tin. A metal plaque on the figure states that Carlton carved it in 1926. The head is detachable. Carlton, a loner, was at one time a caretaker at St. John's Episcopal Church in Deadwood, South Dakota. H: 63¹/₂″; W: 18″. (Private Collection)

FIG. 46. (RIGHT) *Janus-faced root fantasy*. Anonymous. Varnished, bead eyes. Found in Vermont. Late 19th century. H: 14¹/₂″. (Private Collection)

FIG. 47. (LEFT) *Man* by Hugh David Ellington. Iron, probably forged rather than cast, and showing evidence of extensive handwork. The artist is said to have been a blacksmith who lived in Virginia, but the piece was found in Oxonville, Maryland. For so small a figure, the feeling of powerful strength and the fine detail are extraordinary. Late 19th century. H: 10″. (Private Collection)

FIG. 48. (OPPOSITE) *Welder.* Anonymous. Obviously the work of an accomplished welder, this hollow figure was formed by heating, hammering and welding sheet steel. Found in a California flea market, it is thought to have been made in the 1930s. H: 20½″. (Private Collection)

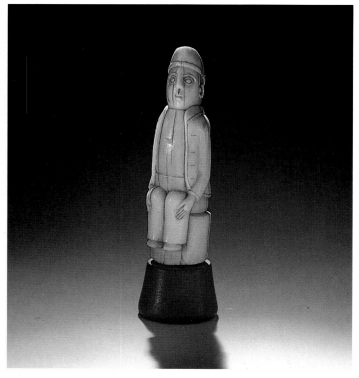

FIG. 49. (ABOVE LEFT) *Athlete.* Anonymous. Wood with polychrome. Ca. 1920–30. H: 6¹/₂″. (Collection of Alice Quinn)

FIG. 50. (ABOVE RIGHT) *Scrimshaw sculpture of a man.* Anonymous. 19th century. H: 3⁵/₈″. (Collection of Howard and Catherine Feldman)

FIG. 51. (LEFT) *Scarecrow.* Anonymous. Wood, paint, rubber, metal. This assemblage of found materials once hung in an apple orchard in Maine. Total H: 26″; W: 20″; head: 9³/₄″. (Private Collection)

FIG. 52. (OPPOSITE) *Telamon.* Anonymous. Wood, crackled varnish. Origin unknown. A telamon is a male version of a caryatid. This unusually proportioned but nonetheless graceful one was evidently meant to support a lamp or vase. The style of the base suggests the 1920s; it could be, however, as early as the 19th century. H: 33″. (Private Collection)

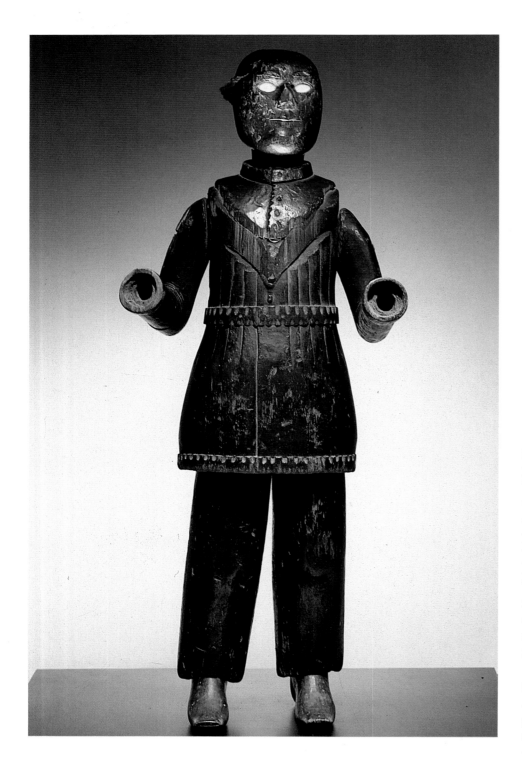

FIG. 53. (LEFT) *Jesuit frontier priest*. Anonymous. Yellow poplar, bear fur, shell eyes. This figure could be as early as the late 17th century. Found in northern Indiana, and once used as a tobacconist's counter display. Because of the facial features, the figure is thought to have been carved by an Indian but intended to portray a white man. The arms are articulated (the hands are missing), the boots and trousers removable. The hair is pegged in the tonsure style associated with Jesuits. H: 21½"; W: 8"; D: 4". (Courtesy William Greenspon)

FIG. 54. (OPPOSITE) *Horse and rider*. Anonymous. Wood with polychrome, glass eyes. Found in New England, this stylized carving with articulated arms was probably intended as a child's toy, though its condition suggests that it was never used. Late 19th, early 20th century. H: 14½"; W: 13"; D: 4". (Silverstein Collection)

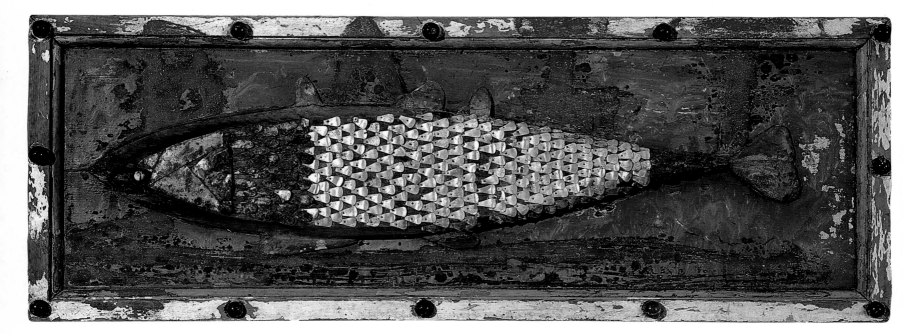

2

UTILITARIAN

THE OBJECTS in this chapter were intended to serve a utilitarian function that could just as easily have been accomplished with a basic, plain, unembellished form. However, the impulse innate in human beings to endow an object with a personal or ceremonial character and spirit has made these works unique. In some instances the function of the object was the springboard to an artistic impulse, as in the case of the fishnet weight (Fig. 57) or the paper-towel holder (Fig. 59). With the musical instrument case (Fig. 81) it was undoubtedly the maker's affection for his instrument that resulted in such an unusual embellishment.

The intentions of the makers of the various objects may have been as different as the objects themselves. It could have been merely a desire for a new pipe that inspired the two female forms (Fig. 60 and p. 7), but more likely it was the shape of the wood that suggested the form. A corncob pipe would have been easy to make and as effective functionally, but hardly as beautiful or as erotically pleasing to hold caressingly in the hand. Some of the objects are obviously shop-related, like the fish sign (Fig. 56), which dates back to an era when literacy was a sometime thing, a fact that inspired shop owners to supplement lettered signs with artistic renderings of their

FIG. 55. *Bait shop sign*. Anonymous. Wood, polychrome, metal can tabs, glass marbles. Used outside a bait shop in the Midwest, this resourceful assemblage simply but effectively announces the shop's goods. Ca. 1930–40. H: 17″; W: 46″; D: 1¹/₂″. (Private Collection; photograph Cheri Eisenberg)

wares. The effectiveness of a dramatic display even in modern times was equally apparent to the owner of the shoe shop that displayed the shoe sculpture (Fig. 58) in its window. Obviously the product of a working environment, the form of the pencil holder and note board (Fig. 73) from an old dress factory is (perhaps unconsciously) dramatically abstract, while the mirror (Fig. 84) from a bunkhouse in Texas celebrates horses. In both instances, the art transcends their utility.

Function was also the intention of the desk (Fig. 86) said to have been made by an ex-slave, and the twig chair (Fig. 90). Both are examples of the inspired use of found materials to make individualized interpretations of traditional furniture styles.

A distinctively minimalist and arresting treatment of a purely functional object has made a powerful image of the glass "catcher's" mask

FIG. 58. (OPPOSITE) *Custom shoemaker's sign.* Anonymous. Wood, leather. The shoemakers in the Foot Culture Orthopedic Shoe Store on West 23rd Street in New York City made this window display themselves. The store went out of business only recently. Ca. 1940. H: 12″; W: 27″; D: 7″. (Private Collection)

FIG. 56. (RIGHT) *Fish shop sign.* Anonymous. Wood with polychrome, tack eyes. Ca. 1850. L: 15″; H: 3¹/₂″; D: 2¹/₂″. (Collection of Helen and Scudder Smith)

FIG. 57. (BELOW) *Fishnet weight.* Anonymous. Cast iron. Though fishnet weights are common, it is rare to find one that is sculpted. Late 19th, early 20th century. L: 36″. (Private Collection)

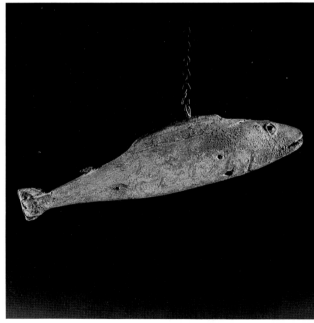

(Fig. 66), while size and eclectic placement of holes to allow air to escape during the cutting of dough have endowed the 18-inch cookie cutter (Fig. 72) with a modern abstract beauty.

Ultimately, whatever the ostensible intended use of these and other objects, whether the love of music and one's own instrument (Figs. 82 and 83) or the need for a ballot box (Fig. 65), the real if hidden reason for their being made is that they afforded their makers an opportunity to create something wonderful: a work of art.

FIG. 59. (LEFT) *Paper-towel holder.* Signed "J. J. Kirk." Wood with polychrome, metal spring. Found in West Virginia. Early 20th century. H: 20″; W: 9″. (Herbert Waide Hemphill, Jr., Collection)

FIG. 60. (ABOVE) *Pipe bowl.* Anonymous. Maple, polychrome. Found in New England. There are indications of stockings and garters on the legs. Late 19th century. H: 8″. (Private Collection)

FIG. 61. (OPPOSITE LEFT) *Coat hanger.* Anonymous. Wood, traces of paint. Found in North Carolina. This surrealistic, whimsical object was carved from a branch stripped of bark and painted. The small holes at the top and bottom show it once was nailed to a wall. Early 20th century. Total L: 16″; hand: 5″. (Courtesy Frederick B. Hanson)

FIG. 62. (OPPOSITE RIGHT) *Tiller.* Anonymous. Weathered wood, wire reinforcements. Found in New England. Although this form is not unique, this example is powerful in its simplicity. Late 19th, early 20th century. H: 16″; W: 12″. (Collection of Ricco-Maresca Gallery)

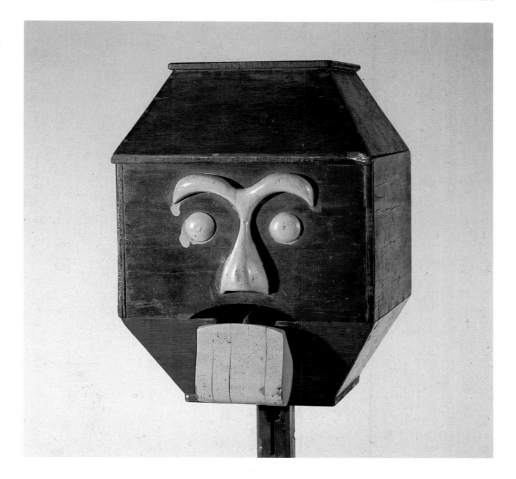

FIG. 63. (OPPOSITE) *Ballot box.* Anonymous. Wood, leather, metal tacks, found objects. Found in Illinois, this box was used in a fraternal order. Early 20th century. H: 13″; W: ³/₄″; D: 12″. (Carl Hammer Gallery; photograph Cheri Eisenberg)

FIG. 64. (ABOVE) *Head of mechanical man* by E. E. Baun. Wood with polychrome and varnish. The mouth drops open as the lid is lifted. Inscribed "January 24, 1938." H: 16¹/₂″; W: 8¹/₂″. (Courtesy William Greenspon)

FIG. 65. (RIGHT) *Ballot box.* Anonymous. Clay. Once used by a fraternal organization, this anthropomorphic ballot box has a removable head. Ca. 1880–1900. H: 9″; W: 6¹/₂″. (The Hall Collection of American Folk and Isolate Art)

FIG. 66. (LEFT) *Glass "catcher's" mask.* Anonymous. Wood. Probably made by the man who wore it to protect his face as he sheared glass from the blower's pipe. His teeth gripped the leather thong to keep the mask in place. 19th century. H: 10½"; w: 7½". (Collection of William Greenspon)

FIG. 67. (BELOW) *Bank.* Anonymous. Cast iron with polychrome. Stamped "1842." Origin unknown. H: 11"; w: 5⅛"; D: 3½". (Collection of Howard and Catherine Feldman)

FIG. 68. (ABOVE) *Mirror.* Anonymous. Wood, varnish, paint, mirror. Found in Connecticut. The bas-relief may have been a portrait. Ca. 1860–65. H: 8¹/₂″; W: 5″. (Marvel Collection)

FIG. 69. (RIGHT) *Watch hutch.* Anonymous. Limestone. Found in Pennsylvania. This work was possibly executed by a tombstone carver. It appears that it once had a hinged door and, of course, a watch. Ca. 1800. H: 12¹/₂″; W: 9″; D: 4³/₄″. (Private Collection)

FIG. 70. (LEFT) *Pipe rack.* Anonymous. Pine with polychrome. The abstraction of the figures and their paper-cutout quality make this once-familiar object exceptional. The rack held long-stem clay pipes. Connecticut. 18th century. H: 27$^1/_2$"; W: 14$^3/_4$"; D: 6". (Private Collection)

FIG. 71. (BELOW) *Andirons.* Anonymous. Wrought iron. Found in New England. Though it was made around the middle of the 19th century, the abstract quality of the design is strikingly modern in effect. H: 18". (Private Collection)

FIG. 72. (BELOW) *Cookie cutter.* Anonymous. Tin. Found in Pennsylvania. This unusually large cookie cutter was very likely used to make giant gingerbread men. Mid-19th century. H: 18″; w: 9″. (Collection of Frank Maresca)

FIG. 73. (RIGHT) *Figurative pencil holder and note board.* Anonymous. Oxidized wood and metal spring. Probably used in a dressmaking factory. The spring device at the waist held pencils. Ca. 1925. H: 58″; w: 24″; D: 1″. (Collection of Roger Ricco)

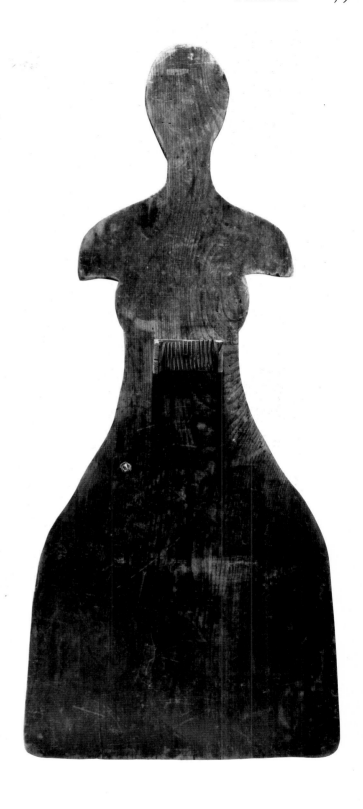

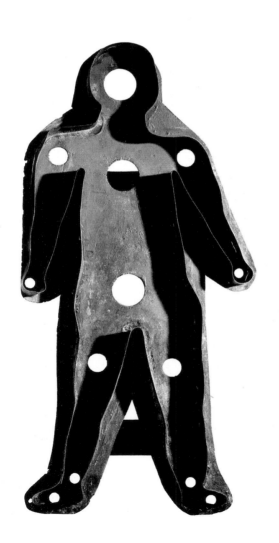

FIG. 74. (OPPOSITE) *Andirons.* Anonymous. Forged iron. Found in Wethersfield, Connecticut. These are said to have been made as a gift for a man who sang in a barbershop quartet. Early 20th century. H: 36″. (Private Collection)

FIG. 75. (RIGHT) *Miniature book box.* Anonymous. Sweet-gum wood with polychrome. Late 19th century. H: 3¹/₂″; w: 4¹/₄″; D: 1¹/₄″. (Collection of Isobel and Harvey Kahn)

FIG. 76. (BELOW) *Snake andirons.* Anonymous. Forged iron. Found in Ohio. First quarter 20th century. Each: H: 13″; w: 11″. (Private Collection)

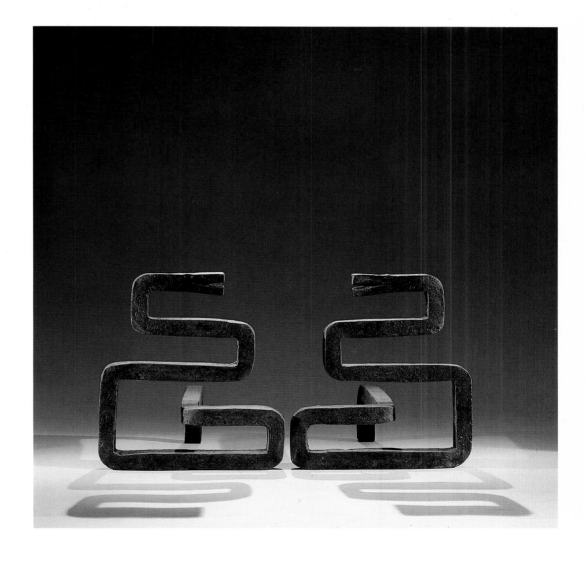

FIG. 77. (LEFT) *Sailor's work ladle.* Anonymous. Maple with varnish. Found in Minnesota, this piece reflects a strong Scandinavian influence. Late 19th century. L: 12"; bowl: 3¹/₂" × 3". (Collection of Timothy and Pamela Hill)

FIG. 78. (BELOW) *Snake door knocker.* Wrought iron, traces of green paint. Found in Pennsylvania. First quarter 19th century. L, head to tail: 11". (Collection of Frank Maresca)

FIG. 79. (ABOVE) *Pincushion holder*. Anonymous. Wood, polychrome. The pincushions would have been in the shoes. The rose and the heart, traditional emblems of love, and the lily and the lamb, symbols of death and resurrection, make this an unusual memorial piece. Late 19th, early 20th century. L: 9″; W: 9″. (Collection of Larry and Gloria Silverstein)

FIG. 80. (RIGHT) *Turkey caller rattle*. Anonymous. Copper, wood, dry corn. Ca. 1900. L: 10¹/₂″; W: 8¹/₂″. (Collection of Lenny, Nancy and Jessica Kislin)

FIG. 81. (LEFT) *Fiddle case.* Anonymous. Wood with polychrome. The carving was probably a stylized portrait of the musician. Early 20th century. L: 30″. (Private Collection)

FIG. 82. (RIGHT) *Guitar.* Anonymous. Wood, metal. Found in New Orleans, this handmade guitar has a photograph of a black man framed under glass on the back and is inscribed with the initials "K.C." 1920. L: 35″; W: 10³/₄″. (Herbert Waide Hemphill, Jr., Collection)

FIG. 83. (OPPOSITE) *Guitar.* Anonymous. Wood with polychrome, tin decoration, wrought-iron pegs and frets, wire strings. Found in Kentucky. This remarkable instrument is built of ³/₄″-thick wood pieces glued together. The peg holes, which are on the face of the neck, not only go all the way down the neck but pierce the sounding box as well. Early 20th century. H: 35″; W: 11″; D: 3″. (Courtesy Cynthia Beneduce; collection of Michael and Gail Mendelson)

FIG. 84. (OPPOSITE AND DETAIL BELOW) *Mirror with horse heads.* Anonymous. Wood, black paint, varnish, mirror. This mirror, found in a Texas bunkhouse, also served as a towel rack. Early 20th century. Overall H: 17½"; W: 24". (*Antiques and the Arts Weekly/ The Newtown Bee*)

FIG. 85. (RIGHT) *Figurative towel rack.* Anonymous. Wood, polychrome. Origin unknown. First half 20th century. H: 8³/₈"; W: 14½"; D: 1½". (Courtesy Marna Anderson's American Folk Art Gallery)

FIG. 86. (LEFT) *Child's desk.* Anonymous. Found wooden parts. Evidently patterned after a formal secretary desk, this interpretation is said to have been made by an ex-slave for use by his child. Found in the South. Mid-19th century. Approximate H: 72″; W: 34″; D: 29″. (Private Collection)

FIG. 87. (OPPOSITE) *Tramp art chest.* Anonymous. Wood, aluminum paint, glass knobs. Tramp art, so called because it was done by itinerants, was usually made of found wood and is ordinarily characterized by ornate, even excessive chip-carved detail. This piece is rare both in its relatively spare use of such detail and in the modernism of its strong graphic design. Ca. 1920. H: 3½′; W: 4′; D: 22″. (Private Collection)

FIG. 88. (LEFT) *Armchair* by Leroy Person. Wood, found furniture parts, red paint. Person made these chairs for his personal use. Assembled from odd pieces of found wood and decorated with deeply engraved linear designs, this chair is almost thronelike in presence. Ca. 1979. H: 38½″; W: 26″; D: 20″. (Collection of Ricco-Maresca Gallery)

FIG. 89. (BELOW) *Pair of red chairs* by Leroy Person. Wood, found furniture parts, red paint. Ca. 1979. H: 33½″; W: 16″; D: 18″. (Collection of Robert Lynch)

LEROY PERSON (1908–85), of North Carolina, was an illiterate sawmill worker who, upon retirement in 1978 and until severely incapacitated by asthma in 1982, created a body of carved wood sculpture, wire sculpture, drawings and furniture. Most of these reflected motifs of his years as a sawmill worker and of the rural area in which he lived.

FIG. 90. (OPPOSITE) *Twig wing chair.* Anonymous. Twigs laid over solid wood frame. Found in Michigan, this is an idiosyncratic version of the more common twig chair. Its geometric pattern is unique, as are its regal dimensions. Ca. 1920–30. H: 56″; W: 28″; D: 28″. (Collection of Ricco-Maresca Gallery; photograph Cheri Eisenberg)

3

PORTRAITURE and FACES

FIG. 91. *Bust of a woman.* Anonymous. Pine, traces of paint. This portrait bust, found in New England, may have been used as a pilothouse figure. Ca. 1850. H: 15″; W: 12″; D: 4″. (Private Collection)

IN GOING through various collections to select objects that met our criteria for this book, we became aware that there were a surprising number that were representations of heads and faces—in other words, portraits.

Some were quite obviously made in the twentieth century, but because the artists are unknown, their significance and intention are difficult to judge, like the fragment (Fig. 137) (possibly of a totem) of a torso whose head is proportionally larger than the hand holding the book; its function is a mystery, as is that of the face in a beam (Fig. 135).

Though there are a large number of twentieth-century portraits that are one of a kind, they are not, as are many of the nineteenth-century busts and portraits, done in keeping with a tradition or particular use. Rather, they have been made for pleasure or diversion, or more likely the artist's need to make art. Vernon Burwell, a prolific living artist, chose a very difficult medium—concrete—to create a diversity of subjects, including animals and full figures. However, his favorite subject seems to be what obviously are portraits of friends and family (Figs. 114 and 115).

With some of the twentieth-century naive sculptors, applied paint or

FIG. 92. (LEFT) *Figurehead.* Anonymous. Wood with polychrome. The small size of this carving suggests it might have been a pilothouse figure. Mid-19th century. H: 15 ¹/₂"; W: 12"; D: 8". (Collection of Howard and Catherine Feldman)

color is an important ingredient in their art, evidently for the purpose of accentuating verisimilitude. It is interesting to compare Burwell's pieces, all of which were made during the last few years, with an anonymous piece (Fig. 111), also in concrete aggregate and polychromed, made in the 1920s or 1930s, which, though naive, seems to be much more traditional in its style.

In the nineteenth century, particularly along the Eastern seaboard, many carvers were employed in shops that produced sculpture commercially. These shops and the carvers, who had no formal art training but undertook carving as a trade, endeavored to supply the needs of the business community of the period, just as the itinerant nineteenth-century "folk" painters painted portraits of household members on order to satisfy a family's desire for memorialization. A commercial carving shop might make tobacconist figures and carve shop signs, show figures and ships' figureheads. Pieces (Figs. 93, 94, 95, 98–101) were produced by carvers of

FIG. 93. (RIGHT) *Ship's figurehead.* Anonymous. Pine with polychrome. Probably from Stonington, Connecticut, this is one of a small number of late-18th-century American figureheads depicting women in period dress. H: 30¹/₂″; W: 15¹/₂″. (Courtesy William Greenspon)

varying degrees of skill and talent. As shop workers, few would have considered themselves sculptors, much less artists.

These carvers were all attempting to do realistic or lifelike interpretations of their subjects, but whether because of commercial expediency or because of a relative lack of skill, detail was often kept to a minimum (Fig. 94). Whatever the reason, there is considerable individual stylization in many such pieces, and they are the ones that have customarily been called primitive or "folk" art.

Another prominent example of objects made by trade workers but much different in both appearance and tradition are the face jugs and other objects made of fired and glazed clay. Sometimes made as an after-work piece, with leftover materials, or as a special commission, these highly stylized sculptures have been something of a tradition among Southern and Ohio pottery workers since before the Civil War. They've been called an assortment of names: slave jugs, face vessels, voodoo pots, grotesque jugs,

FIG. 94. (LEFT AND DETAIL BELOW) *Ship's figurehead* attributed to John W. Mason. Mason was a ship's figurehead carver who worked in Boston. Here he has depicted an Indian maiden. She graced the prow of a coastal ship that was 125 feet long. Ca. 1840. H: 30″; W: 17″; D: 14″. (Courtesy William Greenspon)

plantation pottery and effigy jugs. A good portion of the last are from the Edgefield district of South Carolina, an area noted for the production of utilitarian pottery, particularly during the third quarter of the nineteenth century.

It is worth noting that the creators of these jugs were not in the trade of image making, as were the shop carvers. Their day-to-day work was making household vessels or sewer and building tiles. Yet these workers produced a large body of superb, dramatic sculpture, the artistry of which is all the more remarkable for being in a medium that is difficult to work with.

Whereas some portraits are meant to serve a purpose, like the hat form (Fig. 131), or are egocentric advertising, such as the four heads (Figs. 98–101), some are what might be called "homemade" portraits: the young woman (Fig. 130) and the doll-like versions of Abe and Mary Todd Lincoln (Fig. 128). And though he called them dolls, Calvin Black's performing figures, for all that they resemble one another like sisters, were meant to be portraits of women whom Black knew or admired.

Like the modern artists skilled in abstraction, what the naive or primitive artist does is catch not so much the actuality as the essence of the person portrayed.

FIG. 95. (RIGHT) *Bust of William Seward* signed "J. Bowers, 1861, New York City." Seward was U.S. senator from New York when this was carved. He later served under Lincoln as secretary of state. H: 16″; W: 13¹/₂″; D: 10″. (Private Collection)

FIG. 96. (LEFT) *Bust of Admiral Dewey.* Anonymous. Pine with polychrome. Found in New England. Dewey's role in winning the battle of Manila Bay made him a national hero. Ca. 1898. H: 16″; W: 11″; D: 9″. (Courtesy William Greenspon)

FIG. 97. (BELOW) *Bust of a young man.* Anonymous. Pine with polychrome. Ca. 1880–90. H: 20″; W: 16″; D: 8¹/₂″. (Private Collection)

FIGS. 98–101. (OPPOSITE) *Heads of four men.* Anonymous. Pine with polychrome. Thought to be portraits of the founders of a corporation in Albany, New York, who were probably related to one another. The weathering suggests they were mounted under a gable in front of a building. Ca. 1875. H: 19″; W: 10″; D: 9″. (Courtesy William Greenspon)

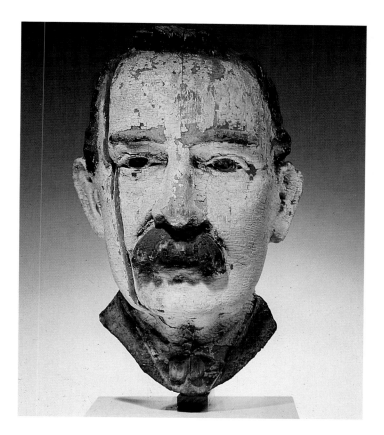
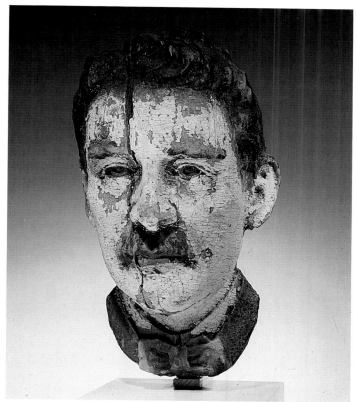
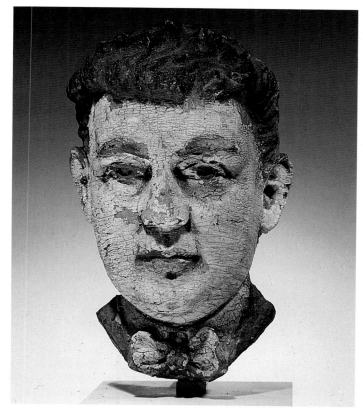
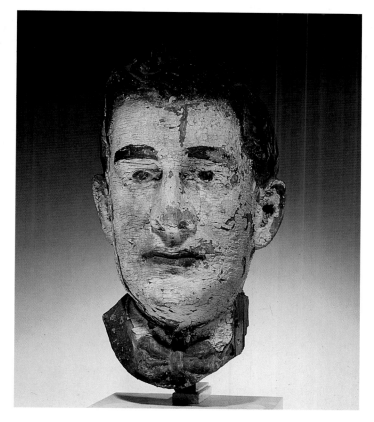

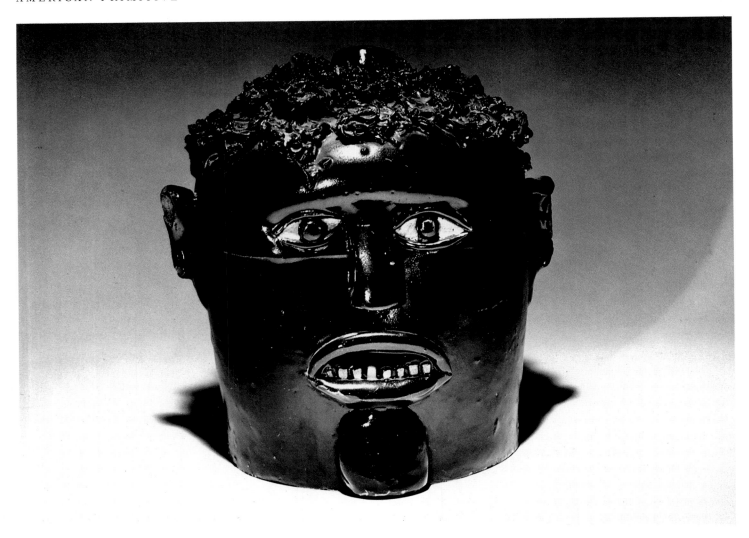

FIG. 102. (ABOVE) *Face jug.* Anonymous. Ohio. Glazed clay. This jug was evidently presented to a member of an Odd Fellows lodge, for inscribed on it is the following: "F L T Martin Schmart 7416 Chillicothe Street, Portsmouth." Ca. 1900. H: 9½". (Collection of Timothy and Pamela Hill)

FIG. 103. (LEFT) *Head of a man.* Anonymous. Glazed clay. Found in Ohio. Late 19th century. H: 9". (Private Collection)

FIG. 104. (RIGHT) *Face jug.* Anonymous. Glazed clay. Found in a basement in Akron, Ohio. Face jugs done as busts are relatively uncommon. Ca. 1870. H: 12¹/₂″. (The Hall Collection of American Folk and Isolate Art)

FIG. 105. (BELOW) *Face jug.* Anonymous. Glazed clay. Found in Georgia. Early 20th century. H: 12¹/₂″. (The Hall Collection of American Folk and Isolate Art)

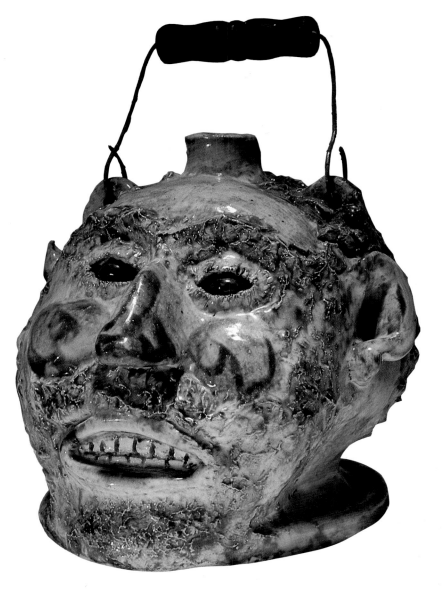

FIG. 106. (LEFT) *Face jug.* Anonymous. White stoneware, cobalt decoration. From an area near Zanesville, Ohio. Ca. 1870–80. H: 8¹/₂″. (Private Collection)

FIG. 107. (BELOW) *Face jug.* Anonymous. Stoneware, alkaline glaze. Found in the Edgefield district of South Carolina, an area noted for pottery making. Ca. 1860. H: 3³/₄″. (Courtesy Michael and Julie Hall)

FIG. 108. (RIGHT) *Face jug.* Anonymous. Clay, black and alkaline glazes. Another jug by the same hand is in the collection of the Ohio Historical Society. Late 19th century. H: 10″. (Collection of George Meyer)

FIG. 109. (BELOW) *Face jug.* Anonymous. Clay, brown glaze. The depiction of a white man on a face jug is unusual. Late 19th century. H: 10″. (Collection of George Meyer)

FIG. 110. (OPPOSITE) *Portrait of a black man* by P. W. McAdam. Dated February 16, 1925. Fired clay, brown slip glaze. Found in Ripley, Mississippi. The hollow construction and the vent holes in the ears and nose indicate that P. W. McAdam probably worked as a potter or kiln worker. H: 16″; W: 8½″; D: 10″. (Private Collection)

FIG. 111. (RIGHT) *Head of a man*. Anonymous. Aggregate of stone and concrete, modeled and carved with polychrome. Found in Pennsylvania. Ca. 1920–30. H: 14″; W: 8″; D: 6½″. (Courtesy Ricco-Johnson Gallery)

FIG. 112. (BELOW) *Sewer-tile bust*. Anonymous. Glazed tile clay. Stamped on the back: "Camp Thompson Sewer Tile Works, Chicago" along with the address: "164 East Adams Street." Stamped on the front three times: "Wm. M. Dee, Esq." Late 19th century. H: 5½″. (The Hall Collection of American Folk and Isolate Art)

FIG. 113. (ABOVE) *Head of a man*. Anonymous. Limestone. Found in Bloomington, Indiana. This head bears a resemblance to African carvings from Sierra Leone. Late 19th century. H: 6³/₄″. (Collection of Frank Maresca)

FIG. 114. (BELOW) *Bust of a man.* 1980–83. H: 24″. (Collection of Geoffrey Holder)

FIG. 115. (RIGHT) *Bust of a lady in a red hat.* 1980–83. H: 28″. (Collection of Geoffrey Holder)

Both by VERNON BURWELL. Concrete with polychrome. Burwell, elderly and retired, lives in rural North Carolina. Much of his work is based on biblical figures, black folk heroes and local characters, but he is also given to making exotic—or imaginary—animals. His work was featured in a show, "Southern Visionary Art," at the Reynolds Gallery in Winston-Salem, North Carolina.

FIG. 116. (OPPOSITE) *Possum Trot Fantasy Theatre dolls* by Calvin Black. Ca. 1955–72. Three indoor figures (L to R): *Evonne* H: 47″; *Charlene* H: 34″; *Miss Jeanne Barlow* H: 41″. (Collection of Frank Maresca)

FIG. 117. (RIGHT) *Rhoda on a bicycle.* An outdoor figure. H: 45″. (Private Collection)

CALVIN BLACK, Tennessee-born (1903–72), settled in Yermo, California, in 1953 after his youthful travels with carnivals and circuses and a try at gold prospecting. He and his wife, Ruby, set up a rock shop in the desert there, and to attract attention to it, Black built a wind-driven merry-go-round which whirled several articulated dolls that Ruby Black dressed in cut-down cast-off clothing. Inside the shop Black built his Possum Trot Fantasy Theatre with a stage full of dolls animated to perform a variety of acts, from running a sewing machine to riding a bicycle. All the dolls were women, all had names, and many were equipped with cassette players and tapes on which Black, using a falsetto voice, had recorded provocative remarks and songs he himself had written, lyrics as well as music. These and the hand-painted signs, lavishly hung both inside and outside the shop and theatre, were expressively typical of Black's unselfconscious, naively sardonic wit.

The dolls, though similar in construction, had distinctive personalities. Those that stayed inside remained pristine, but those outside on the merry-go-round were so ravaged by heat and wind that they were transmogrified into eerie, fetishlike figures. After Ruby Black's death in 1982, Possum Trot was dismantled, and dolls and signs scattered.

FIG. 118. (LEFT) *Charlotte* by Calvin Black. An outdoor figure. It was once attached to a wind-powered carousel. H: 43". (Collection of Frank Maresca)

FIG. 119. (ABOVE) *Doll head* by Calvin Black. H: 15 1/2″. (Courtesy Mr. and Mrs. Clune Walsh)

FIG. 120. (RIGHT) *Possum Trot totem* by Calvin Black. Wood with polychrome. This was one of two totems that were used outside as part of the Possum Trot environment. H: 7′ 5″; W: 8 1/2″; D: 8 1/2″. (Private Collection)

FIG. 121. (OPPOSITE) *Unfinished doll head* by Calvin Black. Wood, traces of black paint. H: 12¹/₂″. (Collection of Frank Maresca)

FIG. 122. (RIGHT) *Head of an articulated figure* by Clark Coe. Wood with polychrome and metal. This head is a fragment from one of several articulated figures that together formed an "environment" in Killingworth, Connecticut. The movements of the figures, both animal and human, were powered by a water wheel. Ca. 1910. H: 13″. (Collection of George Meyer)

FIG. 123. (BELOW) *Head of a woman*. Anonymous. Limestone. Gravestone fragment, found in New Jersey. First quarter 19th century. H: 4¹/₂″. (Collection of Nancy Abraham)

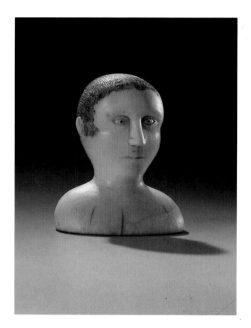

FIG. 124. (LEFT) *Torso of a child holding her pet.* Anonymous. Sandstone. Thought to be a gravestone figure. There is some debate about the origin of this sculpture, which, though found in America, shows a strong Scandinavian influence. Ca. 1800. H: 23″. (Private Collection)

FIG. 125. (BELOW) *Scrimshaw bust of a young man.* Anonymous. Whale ivory, incised details with ink. 19th century. H: 2³/₄″. (Collection of Howard and Catherine Feldman)

FIG. 126. (LEFT) *Coal face.* Anonymous. Anthracite coal. Found in Pennsylvania. Carvings in coal are not uncommon, but such a sensitive and individualistic example is. Ca. 1870–80. H: 8³/₄″; W: 7″. (Marvel Collection)

FIG. 127. (RIGHT) *Stone portrait head.* Anonymous. Found in the South. The date and use of this head remain a mystery. H: 8″; W: 6¹/₂″; D: 1³/₄″. (Private Collection)

FIG. 128. (OPPOSITE) *Abraham and Mary Todd Lincoln.* Anonymous. Wood with polychrome, fabric. A commemorative piece inspired by the fiftieth anniversary of Lincoln's death. Ca. 1915–16. H: 21″. (Courtesy Kelter-Malcé Antiques)

FIG. 129. (RIGHT AND DETAIL ABOVE) *Portrait of a loved one.* Anonymous. Mahogany, red paint, varnish, mirror. Possibly a shipboard carving and most likely given to the woman depicted as a token of love. Late 19th century. H: 10¹/₂″. (Marvel Collection)

FIG. 130. (OPPOSITE) *Bust of a young woman.* Anonymous. Wood with polychrome. A tag affixed to the bottom of this piece describes its origin: "Carved by a farmer in Barton, Vermont. He died two years later and his wife sold it to a local antique shop." Ca. 1930. H: 13½"; W: 6½"; D: 6½". (Private Collection)

FIG. 131. (ABOVE) *Haberdasher's hat form.* Anonymous. Chased copper, tin lining. Found in Brooklyn in an area of copper pot manufacturers, this form was very likely a window display piece. First quarter 20th century. H: 14½"; W: 6"; D: 9". (Private Collection)

FIG. 132. (RIGHT) *Apothecary display head.* Anonymous. Wood, tin tongue, rubber ears. It was not uncommon for apothecaries to display similar heads in their windows with pills on their tongues. This one, in view of its weathered condition, may have spent more time outdoors than in. Believed to be early 20th century. H: 11"; W: 6½"; D: 6". (Collection of Roger Ricco)

FIG. 133. (OPPOSITE) *Phrenology head.* Anonymous. Wood with penciled markings. Phrenology, a pseudoscience, posited the theory that mental ability and character could be determined from a study of the conformation of the skull and its bumps. This head, found in Maine, is one of the few American phrenology heads in wood known to exist. Mid-19th century. H: $9^{1}/_{2}''$. (Collection of Kenneth and Ida Manko)

FIG. 134. (RIGHT) *Cast-iron head with glass marble eyes.* Anonymous. Found in Pennsylvania. The back of the head is open to reveal a brain made of lead. Late 19th century. H: $4^{1}/_{2}''$. (Collection of Frank Maresca)

FIG. 135. (BELOW) *Relief of a man's face.* Anonymous. Carved into a section of a beam. Found in upstate New York. Ca. 1930–40. H of beam: 24''; W: 10''. (Private Collection)

FIG. 136. (LEFT) *Head totem.* Anonymous. Wood with polychrome. Once used as an outdoor barbershop pole. Ca. 1940. H: 90". (Private Collection)

FIG. 137. (OPPOSITE) *Fragment of a man with a book.* Anonymous. Wood with polychrome. Carved from a tree trunk that subsequently was hollowed out by insect erosion, it may have been part of a larger totem. H: 29½"; W: 11"; D: 9". (Private Collection)

4

WEATHERVANES and WHIRLIGIGS

WEATHERVANES, once omnipresent on barns in rural areas and on church steeples, public buildings and sometimes private homes, perhaps more than any other genre of American art, manifest the wide range of original imagination, sensitivity to form and ingenuity that is characteristic of much American naive sculpture.

The most prevalent weathervanes were factory produced, and generally were made of two mirror-image sheets of copper that had been hammered into molds, soldered together and then gilded. Factories offered an extensive choice of subjects, such as running horses and other farm animals, several of which could be had in various sizes, and any of which could be ordered through a catalogue and shipped by mail. It was not at all unusual for factories to copy one another's patterns or rare for two manufacturers to produce virtually identical vanes.

Factory-made weathervanes, like many other objects duplicated in large numbers in a shop but involving a certain amount of handwork, are commonly presented under the heading of "Americana and Folk Art," and they now constitute a significant area of collecting in that field.

The vanes illustrated here, however, though they may depict some of

FIG. 138. *Prancing horse weathervane.* Anonymous. Wood, heavily weathered metal tail, metal repairs. Late 19th century. H: 18″; L: 28″. (Private Collection)

the same subjects that were popular in factory-made vanes, are each a unique sculpture and singular concept. Most were devised, in all likelihood, by the farmer who used them or by someone in the local area with a particular skill or special ingenuity, like a woodworker, blacksmith or tinsmith. The angel Gabriel (Fig. 154) appears to have been just that kind of vane. It at one time surmounted a public building and so may have been commissioned, but not another like it has ever been seen, so it very well may have been made by a blacksmith who never produced the same form again. Eagles were a standard subject for factory-produced vanes, but few have the striking originality of the one assembled out of found materials (Fig. 147), or of the cow Fig. 146.

Because they had to be seen from afar, weathervanes had sharp, distinct silhouettes, so that when seen against the sky they presented an imme-

FIG. 139. (OPPOSITE) *Running horse weathervane*. Anonymous. Pine, traces of paint, heavily weathered. This vane depicting a horse running flat out is similar to one that has an Indian astride it in the Abby Aldrich Rockefeller Folk Art Collection. Ca. 1880–90. H: 9″; L: 30″. (Courtesy Mr. and Mrs. Robert P. Marcus Collection)

FIG. 140. (RIGHT) *Horse weathervane*. Anonymous. Wood with polychrome. The banner on which this fully rounded horse stands has a fish cutout at its tail. Late 19th, early 20th century. H: 16¹/₂″; L: 50″. (Private Collection)

diately recognizable form, like the flying-goose vane (Fig. 152) by Elmer Crowell or Albert Zahn's running dog (Fig. 161). It was not unusual for vanes to have cutout motifs through which light could pass, like the sheet-metal rooster (Fig. 143) or the fish cutout in the banner on which a horse stands (Fig. 140).

Vanes like these were apt to have been made of transitory materials, such as wood or tin, or a combination of both. Hence, unlike copper vanes, which withstand the elements for decades, these individually produced vanes were much more susceptible to the assaults of time and the elements, which in many cases not only altered but dramatically and aesthetically enhanced them. There is no doubt that the parrot (Fig. 149) and the prancing horse (Fig. 138) have acquired a certain drama they might not have had when new.

Relatives of the weathervane, because they, too, were made to face the wind, whirligigs have something of the aspect of a toy. However, they were not designed only to amuse; they also served as indicators of the strength of the wind. Early whirligigs—those of the nineteenth century—almost always depicted the human form, usually as a caricature or mockery of a figure of authority. However dignified such figures looked when still, like the policeman (Fig. 175) or the Hessian soldier (Fig. 168), they lost all their poise when forced to flail their arms helplessly in the wind.

Twentieth-century whirligigs are markedly different from the earlier ones, and often are more elaborate, with one or more figures being forced to perform some sort of chore when the wind became stiff, like the two men who had to saw ice (Fig. 179).

Ordinarily, whirligigs were positioned on a post outdoors in front of the house or on a fence, where they could face the prevailing wind. However, there have been instances where a whirligig was both weather-vane *and* whirligig, like the Uncle Sam on a bicycle (Fig. 164) and the bicycle rider (Fig. 165). Both were once affixed on roofs, and when their propellers caught the wind, their legs went into action.

Thousands of factory-produced weathervanes still exist, but, like the exceptional whirligig, relatively few one-of-a-kind vanes have managed to escape destruction. Those that have attest to the ingenuity, resourceful-ness, imagination and natural sense of design as well as to the spontaneity and creative independence that are characteristic of much American naive sculpture.

FIG. 141. (BELOW) *Horse weathervane frag-ment.* Anonymous. Sheet metal. Found in New England. Late 19th century. L: 30″. (Private Collection)

FIG. 142. (OPPOSITE) *Running hound weathervane.* Anonymous. Wood with polychrome. Found in Maine. Late 19th, early 20th century. H: 9″; L: 25″. (Blumert-Fiore Collection)

FIG. 143. (LEFT) *Rooster weathervane.*
Anonymous. Sheet metal, traces of paint.
Found in New Paltz, New York. Late 18th,
early 19th century. H: 12″; W: 12″. (Herbert
Waide Hemphill, Jr., Collection)

FIG. 144. (BELOW) *Rooster weathervane.*
Anonymous. Wood, metal, polychrome.
Ca. 1860. H: 21″; W: 19″. (Courtesy *Antiques
and the Arts Weekly/The Newtown Bee*)

FIG. 145. (ABOVE) *Cow weathervane*. Anonymous. Hollow tin body with traces of polychrome. A very similar vane by the same hand is known to exist. Early 20th century. Approximate H: 28″; L: 41″; D: 3″. (Courtesy Ricco-Johnson Gallery)

FIG. 146. (RIGHT) *Cow weathervane*. Anonymous. Wood, metal bracing, iron horns. Found in upper New York State. Late 19th, early 20th century. H: 31″; L: 21″. (Courtesy William Greenspon)

FIG. 147. (LEFT) *Eagle weathervane*. Anonymous. Wood, metal with polychrome. This weathervane is an assemblage: the carved eagle is perched on a copper ball fitted with piano stool feet and mounted on a wooden arrow put together with odd factory-made parts. Early 20th century. H: 38″; W: 19″; D: 20″. (Private Collection; courtesy Ricco-Johnson Gallery)

FIG. 148. (BELOW) *Fish weathervane*. Anonymous. Tin over wood, polychrome, bottle cap eyes. Ca. 1940–50. H: 6¼″; W: 28¾″. (Collection of Frank Maresca)

FIG. 149. (OPPOSITE) *Parrot weathervane*. Anonymous. Wood, traces of paint, lead weight eyes. The feathering on this unique weathervane was achieved through lamination, an effect enhanced by exposure to the elements. Ca. 1880. Beak to tail: 23″; D: 4″. (Courtesy Helen and Scudder Smith)

FIG. 150. (ABOVE) *Swan weathervane* by Fred Read. Wood, weathered white paint. A photo of Read's barn in Cornish, New Hampshire, taken prior to 1890, shows this swan mounted atop it. Read has been credited with making four such swan weathervanes. Ca. 1880–90. H: 15″; L: 58″. (Private Collection)

FIG. 151. (LEFT) *Stag weathervane.* Anonymous. Sheet metal, iron bracing. Late 19th century. H: 30″; L: 21″. (Private Collection)

FIG. 152. (RIGHT) *Flying goose weather-vane* by Elmer Crowell. Weathered pine. Crowell was a master decoy carver, and this weathervane was at one time affixed to his house in East Harwich, Massachusetts. Ca. 1930–40. H: 13½"; L: 27½". (Private Collection)

FIG. 153. (BELOW) *Sea serpent weather-vane*. Anonymous. Sheet metal, forged-iron gills with polychrome. From Portland, Connecticut. The forged-iron gills are used as counterweights. The vane is crowned by a finial depicting a pineapple leaf, a symbol of friendship. Ca. 1880–90. H: 27", including rod; L: 36". (Private Collection)

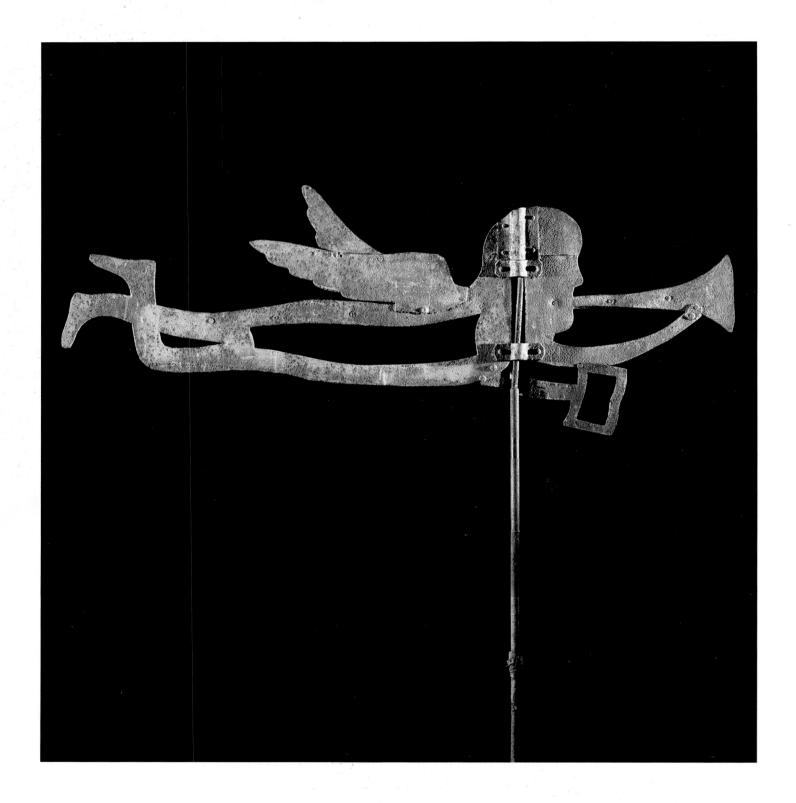

FIG. 154. (OPPOSITE) *Angel Gabriel weathervane.* Anonymous. Sheet metal. A representation of the angel Gabriel blowing his horn, this weathervane once was atop the North Leverett Baptist Church in North Leverett, Massachusetts. 19th century. H: 28″; L: 48″. (Courtesy Helen and Scudder Smith)

FIG. 155. (RIGHT) *Running horse weathervane.* Anonymous. Wood with polychrome. Found in Massachusetts. Ca. 1870–80. L: 28″. (Marvel Collection)

FIG. 156. (BELOW) *Horse and rider weathervane.* Anonymous. Pine, tin, with polychrome. Found in Massachusetts. Ca. 1890. H: 32″; L: 58″. (Collection of Timothy and Pamela Hill)

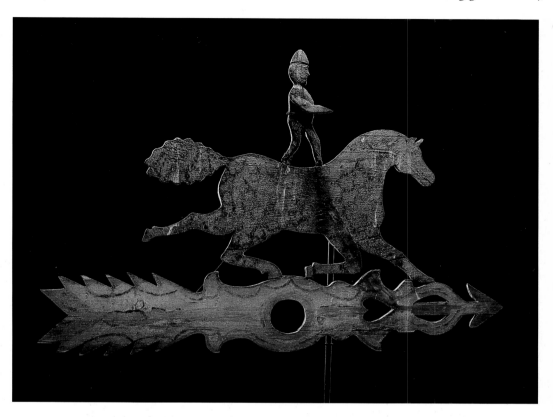

FIG. 157. (OPPOSITE) *Horse weathervane.* Anonymous. Wood, traces of paint, cast-iron arrow. The form resembles that of a Chinese Tang Dynasty horse. Mid-19th century. H: 21″; L: 25″. (Patricia Guthman Collection)

FIG. 158. (ABOVE) *Acrobatic rider weathervane.* Anonymous. Wood, metal, wire, traces of paint. This weathervane, unusual in its combination of quite distinctive elements, first surfaced at a central Wisconsin farm estate sale. Late 19th, early 20th century. H: 47″; L: 32″. (Courtesy Richard Levey and Sigrid Christiansen)

FIG. 159. (RIGHT) *Centaur weathervane.* Anonymous. Wood, traces of paint. Found in New York State. Most of the known centaur weathervanes were of copper and were factory made. This is one of the few made in wood and is additionally unique because the upper part of the figure is female. Late 19th century. H: 15″; L: 30″. (Courtesy the Brian Collection)

FIG. 160. (LEFT) *Atlantic salmon weathervane*. Anonymous. Sheet metal. Found in Toms River, New Jersey. Two forms were soldered together, making the body slightly convex. Ca. 1890. H: 11″; L: 32″. (Collection of Steve Miller)

FIG. 161. (BELOW) *Running dog weathervane* by Albert Zahn. Weathered wood. This weathervane was on Zahn's roof in Baileys Harbor, Wisconsin. Zahn was noted for sculptures of birds as well as figures that he claimed were inspired by visions. His work often reflects his Lutheran religious beliefs. Ca. 1925–40. H: 16″; L: 70″; D: 6¹/₂″. (Private Collection)

FIG. 162. (OPPOSITE) *Sawing man weathervane*. Anonymous. Wood, white paint, wire, lead weight. This vane, carved in the semi-round, retains a layer of gold leaf underneath its existing white surface. The porkpie hat dates the piece ca. 1920–30. H: 28″; W: 22″; D: 3″. (Private Collection; photo courtesy Ricco-Johnson Gallery)

FIG. 163. (OPPOSITE) *Basketball player weathervane*. Anonymous. Sheet metal with polychrome. A basketball player became a fit subject for an urban weathervane maker's fancy. Ca. 1930–40. H: 24″; from foot to ball: 26″. (Courtesy *Antiques and the Arts Weekly/The Newtown Bee*)

FIG. 164. (ABOVE) *Uncle Sam whirligig* by Jack Mongillo (1879–1973). Wood, metal, leather, traces of paint. Italian-born Mongillo, who lived most of his life in Salamanca, New York, kept this mammoth whirligig of Uncle Sam delivering the mail atop a barn on his farm. Ca. 1940. H: 30″; L: 44″; D: 55″. (Marvel Collection; photo courtesy Ricco-Johnson Gallery)

FIG. 165. (LEFT) *Bicycle rider weathervane.* Anonymous. Wood, metal. When wind strikes the large wheel, the man's legs pump. Ca. 1880–90. H: 17″; L: 25″. (Courtesy Isobel and Harvey Kahn)

FIG. 166. (BELOW) *Minstrel man whirligig.* Anonymous. Wood, tin, polychrome. The cymbals which functioned as paddles and his waistcoat are constructed of tin. Mid-19th century. H: 13″. (Private Collection)

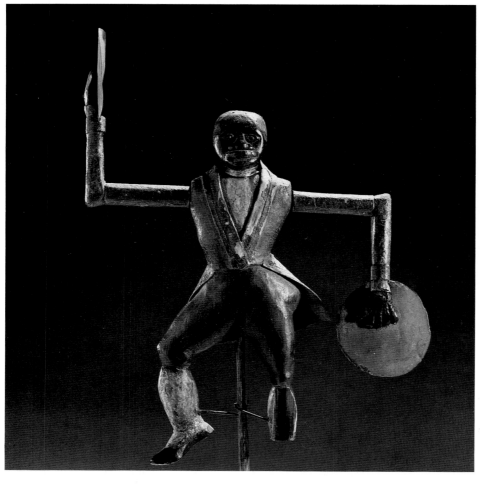

FIG. 167. (BELOW) *Whirligig with an Admiral Nelson hat.* Anonymous. Pine with polychrome. Nelson's dates are 1758–1805, but this armless whirligig was probably made ca. 1880. H: 41″. (Collection of Timothy and Pamela Hill)

FIG. 168. (RIGHT) *Man in a suit whirligig.* Anonymous. Wood with polychrome. Found in New England, this whirligig is unusually large. Late 19th century. H: 42½″. (Private Collection)

FIG. 169. (LEFT) *Hessian soldier whirligig.* Anonymous. Wood, metal. Extreme weathering and the loss of arms and paddles has transfigured this whirligig, giving it a quality different from that intended by its maker. (For simple contrast, see Fig. 167.) Late 19th century. H: 31″. (Private Collection)

FIG. 170. (BELOW) *Whirligig trio.* Anonymous. Wood, traces of paint. Found in Pennsylvania. These three figures were part of a larger construction. Late 19th century. H, each: 11″. (Private Collection)

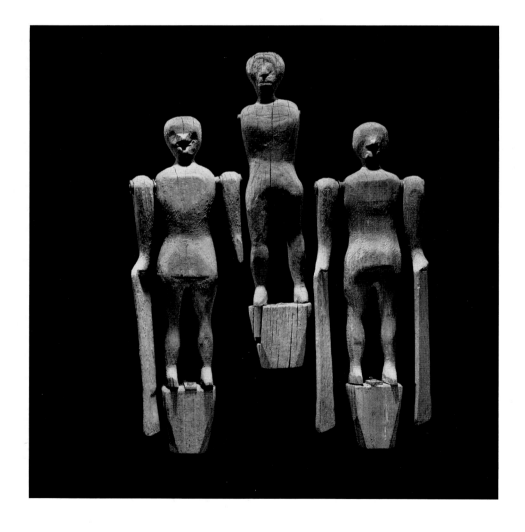

FIG. 171. (ABOVE) *Indian hunter astride a lizard whirligig.* Anonymous. Wood, traces of paint. Inscribed: "Adrian, Ohio." Late 19th century. H, exclusive of paddles: 24″. (Private Collection)

FIG. 172. (RIGHT) *Striding Indian whirligig.* Anonymous. Wood, gesso, tin, paint. Origin unknown. Ca. 1870. H, figure: 15″; H, base to crown: 22″. (Collection of Harvey and Isobel Kahn)

FIG. 173. (LEFT) *Bearded man in a waist-coat whirligig.* Anonymous. Wood with polychrome. Found in New England. This whirligig probably represents a sea captain. Although whirligigs usually portrayed figures of authority, sometimes seeming to mimic their martinet quality, it is rare to find one representing a sea captain. This one has, therefore, something of the quality of a ship's figurehead. 19th century. H: 22½″. (Howard and Catherine Feldman Collection)

FIG. 174. (BELOW) *Trapper whirligig.* Anonymous. Wood with bristle hair and fur, polychrome. An unusually large whirligig found in the Northwest. Early 20th century. H: 27″. (Brian Collection)

FIG. 175. (ABOVE) *Walking man whirligig* by Amos Schultz. Pine with polychrome. Amos Schultz lived in Bucks County, Pennsylvania. Ca. 1860. H, exclusive of arms: 18″. (Steve Miller Collection)

FIG. 176. (ABOVE RIGHT) *Policeman whirligig.* Anonymous. White pine with polychrome. Found in New York State. Ca. 1890. H: 21″. (Steve Miller Collection)

FIG. 179. (OPPOSITE) *Two men sawing ice.* Anonymous. Wood with polychrome, metal. Probably a whirligig with a missing propeller, but possibly a crank toy. The figures bent to the waist and the saw worked up and down. Origin unknown. Early 20th century. H: 16″; W: 10″; D: 4¹/₂″. (Private Collection)

FIG. 177. (ABOVE) *Man in a bowler hat whirligig.* Anonymous. Wood with polychrome. Origin unknown. Late 19th century. H: 23″. (Marvel Collection)

FIG. 178. (RIGHT) *Hessian soldier whirligig.* Anonymous. Wood, tin, traces of paint. Origin unknown. The unusually disproportionate relationship of the figure to the paddles suggests that this weathered soldier must at one time have been mounted on a pole. 19th century. H, figure: 16″; overall extension: 39″. (Collection of Harvey and Isobel Kahn)

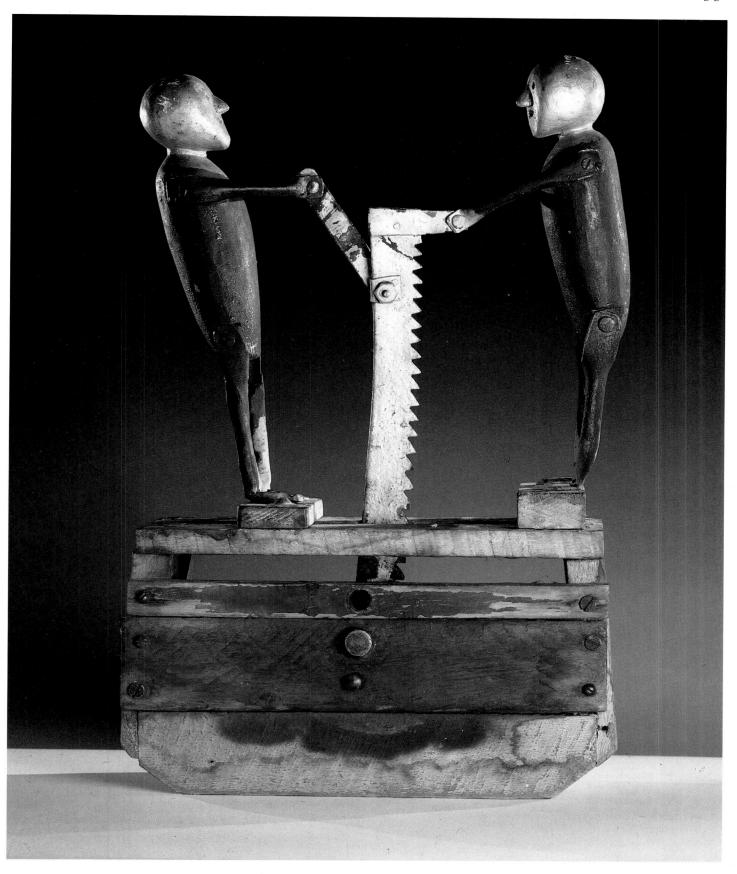

5

ARTICULATED FIGURES

FIG. 180. *Limberjack.* Anonymous. Wood with polychrome, metal, cloth, mother-of-pearl eyes. Found in Buffalo, New York. The arms of this figure are springs, so that when it is made to jump, they move. Late 19th century. H: 16½". (Marvel Collection)

WHEN SMALL sculptures of human figures began to be made for amusement rather than worship, very likely the next development was giving them movable or articulated limbs in order to make them simulate human activities. The apogee of articulated figures was reached in the skillfully crafted automata of seventeenth-, eighteenth- and nineteenth-century Europe, which contained clock mechanisms that controlled their actions. The tin windup and battery-operated plastic ones are their descendants. However, the most artistically intriguing articulated toys are the personally sculpted ones whose antics are brought into play by a manipulating hand, that of the maker or owner.

The articulated toys that seemed to inspire unusually dramatic little sculptures were the limberjacks. These were loosely jointed figures that had a stick or wire attached to the center of the back with which they could be made to swing their arms, tap their feet and even do acrobatics in time to music. A skilled manipulator could use them with a springboard, tapping out the rhythm with his or her fingers, or else make them dance on a tabletop or floor (Figs. 181, 182, 191 and 194). Occasionally, the limberjack (Fig. 180) was too large to be controlled by hand and would instead be

FIG. 181. (LEFT) *Limberjack couple.* Anonymous. Wood with polychrome, metal, tack eyes, fabric hat. Origin unknown. Limberjacks with two figures are rare. Late 19th century. H, of figures: 11″. (Courtesy Isobel and Harvey Kahn)

attached to a springboard in a manner that allowed the entertainer to play an instrument and at the same time make his doll dance by tapping the board with his foot.

Not quite so versatile but still fascinating are other little sculptures animated by either a squeeze-release or a push-pull mechanism (Figs. 189 and 190). The boxing toy (Fig. 200) is particularly intriguing because of its subject matter and the variety of figures put into motion by a crank-and-gear mechanism.

Chances are that these figures, all of which were intended to amuse — either as dancing dolls or, like Figs. 185 and 188, simply, in spite of their

FIG. 182. (OPPOSITE) *Articulated dancing figure.* Anonymous. Wood, traces of paint. The screw-eye joining on this figure contributes to the total design. The nut in its chest was once attached to a metal rod that extended from the back. Late 19th century. H: 11″. (Private Collection)

somewhat unfriendly appearance, as dolls to play with—were made either by someone in the home or by a local carver. Most are from rural areas, where more sophisticated entertainment was either not available or too costly.

Several of the figures depicted blacks, as did the minstrel shows of the late nineteenth century and very early twentieth century, but since the majority of them are anonymous, it is impossible to ascertain if their creation is linked to any racial group. Still, a great number of the nondancing articulated figures show such a strong stylistic resemblance to African sculpture that it seems safe to assume they were made by blacks as dolls for their children (Figs. 185 and 188).

In any event, although intended as objects of amusement, a remarkable diversity of artistic sculptural invention has been achieved in these small figures.

FIG. 183. (LEFT) *Pair of articulated figures.* Anonymous. Wood, polychrome, cloth, beads, fur, glass bead eyes. These two figures are hollow and their heads are flexible. Their face decoration shows the influence of African masks. 20th century. H, of male: 11 1/2″; female: 10 1/2″. (Courtesy Isobel and Harvey Kahn)

FIG. 184. (ABOVE) *Pair of dolls, man and woman*. Anonymous. Wood with polychrome, fabric, buttons. The abstraction of the features shows a direct connection to African masks. The clothes suggest mid to late 19th century. H: 10″. (Private Collection)

FIG. 185. (RIGHT) *Male figure*. Anonymous. Wood, traces of paint, blue glass bead eyes. The arms are articulated. Found in New England, but showing strong African influence. Late 19th, early 20th century. H: 14″. (Collection of Frank Maresca)

FIG. 186. (FAR RIGHT) *Articulated figure*. Anonymous. Wood with polychrome, metal buttons. The arms of this figure are missing. Indications of lip scarification emphasize the strong African quality of this figure. Late 19th century. H: 12″. (Private Collection)

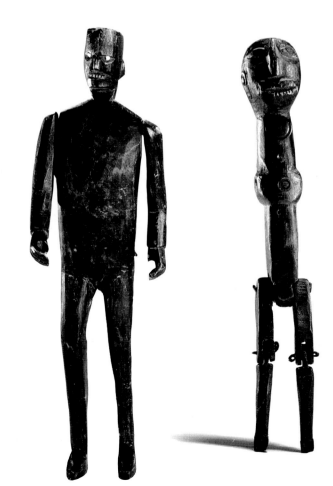

FIG. 187. (LEFT) *Limberjack.* Anonymous. Wood, copper, hair, pearl buttons. The legs of this figure are missing. Its beard is made of bear hair. Southern origin. 19th century. H: 8½". (Courtesy William Greenspon)

FIG. 188. (BELOW LEFT) *Articulated figure.* Anonymous. Wood. The ears are incised. The figure has a smooth, handled quality, suggesting it was probably a doll, not a dancing figure. Ca. 1870–90. H: 9½". (Private Collection)

FIG. 189. (BELOW RIGHT) *Push-pull toy.* Anonymous. Wood, polychromed. Found in Virginia. Ca. 1900. H: 18"; when extended, 20". (Courtesy Isobel and Harvey Kahn)

FIG. 190. (OPPOSITE) *Jumping jack.* Anonymous. Wood. When the poles are squeezed from below, the figure dances and flips over. Late 19th century. H: 13"; D, platform: 12". (Collection of Allan and Ellen Cober)

FIG. 191. (OPPOSITE) *Limberjack.* Anonymous. Wood with polychrome, animal hair, metal rod. An unusually elegant figure. Very few limberjacks of this quality have survived. Late 19th century. H, figure: 13³/₄″; L, paddle: 21¹/₂″. (Blumert-Fiore Collection)

FIG. 192. (RIGHT) *Articulated dancing figure.* Anonymous. Wood, leather, metal. The head and body are covered with leather and decorated with tack buttons and eyes. Ca. 1875–1900. H: 14″. (Blumert-Fiore Collection)

FIG. 193. (ABOVE RIGHT) *Articulated dancing figure.* Anonymous. Wood with polychrome, cloth, bristle. Note the two pouches on his belt. Late 19th century. H: 11″. (Courtesy Isobel and Harvey Kahn)

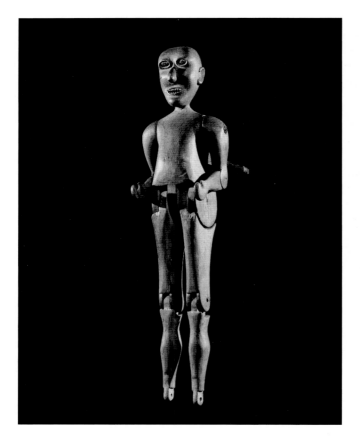

FIG. 194. (ABOVE LEFT) *Articulated figure.* Anonymous. Wood. Found in Pennsylvania. A figure of quite sophisticated design, it has a wooden handle rather than a spring attached to its back. 20th century. H: 15″. (Courtesy Ricco-Maresca Gallery)

FIG. 195. (ABOVE RIGHT) *Articulated figure.* Anonymous. Wood. From Wisconsin. Similar to limberjacks in construction, this figure is an Ojibwa Indian doll that was used in storytelling ceremonies. It was held in the hand in such a way that thumb and forefinger functioned as its arms. Mid-19th century. H: 12½″. (Private Collection)

FIG. 196. (LEFT) *Indian doll.* Anonymous. Wood with polychrome, fabric, beads. The headband once held feathers. Origin unknown. Late 19th, early 20th century. H: 13″. (Marna Anderson Gallery of American Folk Art)

FIG. 197. (RIGHT) *Acrobats.* Anonymous. Wood, darkened with pencil. This man and woman share the same pair of arms. They may have at one time been suspended between two squeeze poles. Early 20th century. H, each figure: 6″. (Private Collection)

FIG. 198. (BELOW) *Articulated toy.* Anonymous. Wood with polychrome metal bell. Multijointed, these figures were put into motion through the use of a hand-operated crank. Ca. 1900. H: 29″; W: 22″; D: 16″. (Collection of George Meyer)

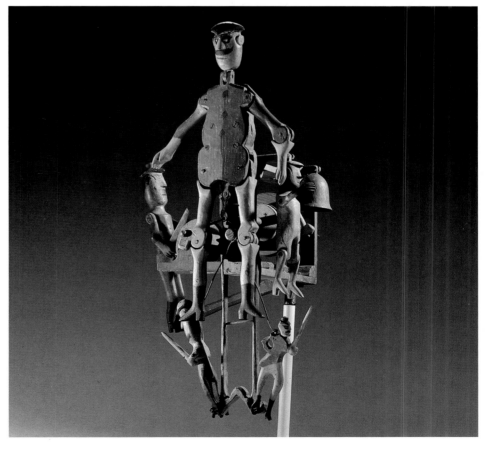

FIG. 199. (LEFT) *Articulated dancing figures* by Charlie Fields. Wood, paint, metal; plastic toy dog. Fields, a.k.a. Cedar Creek Charlie, won national notoriety for his house, which was completely painted inside and out—contents included—with polka dots. He lives in Virginia. Ca. 1960–70. H: 15″; L, platform: 27″; W: 11″. (Herbert Waide Hemphill, Jr., Collection)

FIG. 200. (OPPOSITE) *Boxing-match crank toy.* Anonymous. Wood, cloth, metal, paper, thread, paint. Thought to have been made in Massachusetts, where it was originally found, this toy, when wound, shows a black man boxing a white man; the dog goes up the pole, the rooster tips and the wheels spin. Ca. 1920–30. H: 27″; W: 23″; D: 15″. (Herbert Waide Hemphill, Jr., Collection)

6

DECOYS

IN THE HUNTING and fishing world, the word "decoy" might be considered synonymous with the word "siren," the purpose of decoys being to entice a particular species of bird or fish into the range of the hunter's or fisherman's weapon with a sculpted replica or "impersonator" of that species. Because decoys were devised and used by indigenous Americans long before any Europeans ever discovered, much less explored, this continent, decoy making is considered this country's only truly original folk art.

Once a profession (market gunning) until made illegal in 1913, gunning remains a popular seasonal sport along migratory flyways, and decoys have been produced in large numbers by both factories and individual carvers. Decoy carvers from the beginning endeavored to create decoys that would be as effective as possible in attracting wildfowl or fish, and there were, in a sense, two schools of approach as to how this could be achieved. In the case of ducks and other birds, both individual carvers and factories strove for a high degree of reality and faithful detail. Factory decoys were offered in varying grades, ranging from standard to challenge

FIG. 201. *Pair of swan decoys.* Anonymous. The one in front is in a preening position, the one in the rear in a swimming position. An extraordinary grace and sense of life has been conveyed with a minimal amount of carving. Late 19th century. H: 32"; L: 19". (Private Collection)

FIG. 202. (LEFT) *Shorebird*. Anonymous. Wood with polychrome, metal legs. This decoy, with its abstracted paint pattern, was probably meant to depict a plover. Late 19th, early 20th century. L, tail to bill: 6″. (The Hall Collection of American Folk and Isolate Art)

to premier, with the greatest striving for perfection being lavished on the more expensive birds.

Hunting is a ritualistic sport in which the hunter's concern for his gear often goes beyond its function: hence, just as a hunter might cherish a shotgun for its elegantly engraved adornment, so might he spend more for a decoy he considered to be of better quality. But just as a beautifully fitted shotgun doesn't shoot any better than an undecorated one, it is doubtful that an exact duplicate of a bird is any more successful in attracting a real one flying several hundred feet above a hunter's blind.

Birds see shapes rather than specific details or colors, and the verisimilitude so cherished by some carvers and hunters is not essential for a decoy to be an effective deceiver. Carvers who were aware of this, rather than lavish time on detail, were more given to interpretation and stylization of form. These are the kinds of decoys we show here.

The best of such carvers tended intuitively to select the key elements of

FIG. 203. (RIGHT) *Sea gull*. Probably made by a Maine decoy carver. Cedar, paint, metal wire. Ca. 1890. L: 25″. (Steve Miller Collection)

FIG. 204. (BELOW) *Root-head shorebird, unknown species*. Anonymous. Wood with brown paint, glass bead eyes. Found in Maine. The head is dovetailed into the body, and the selection of the root has given this decoy a "minnow in the throat" look. Late 19th, early 20th century. L: 9″. (Private Collection)

form and coloration of a particular species, reducing the carved form and stance of the bird to its essentials through simplification of both silhouette and paint toning—in essence, abstracting its design. The effect is not unlike great poster art: in a poster, message and composition are pared down to the most basic, instantly identifiable form, the most salient traits being emphasized through stylization. Thus, the eider drake (Fig. 206) displays undulating and fluid curves and bold paint patterns; a working swan (Fig. 213) is given an extremely elongated neck, its body simplified; a stickup gull (Fig. 208) is delineated in extreme abstraction; and the swans (Fig. 201), though primitively and minimally carved, still convey life and grace.

Fish decoys, unlike bird decoys, were seldom factory produced, and, like bird decoys, are believed to have been first made by early indigenous Americans. They were used almost exclusively in ice or spear fishing, primarily in the Great Lakes areas. Though outlawed in most states in the mid-1920s, ice fishing is still legal, under certain conditions, in Wisconsin, Minnesota and Michigan. For this sport, a hole is cut in the ice over a frozen lake and a simple structure is built over the hole to black out the daylight or reflections from the sky so that the fisherman can peer into unshadowed dark water.

The decoy, weighted with lead and attached to a line tied to a short pole, would be suspended in the water. Holding the pole in one hand, a spear in the other, the fisherman would move the decoy around in a circular or swimming movement to attract fish into range.

Like bird decoys, fish decoys vary in style from approximation to realism. But in both categories, the bird and fish decoys we've selected were made by carvers who obviously felt that as the prey they were to lure was some distance off, it was better to emphasize the essential characteristics of the real birds or fish so they could be readily identified from afar or under adverse conditions. The simplification and stylization necessary to achieve this has resulted in carvings of high sculptural merit.

FIG. 205. (BELOW) *Eider drake*. Attributed to Gus Wilson of Portland, Maine. Cedar. An unusually large decoy. Late 19th, early 20th century. H: 10″; W: 10″; L: 20″. (Steve Miller Collection)

FIG. 206. (OPPOSITE) *Eider drake*. Anonymous. Wood with polychrome. Inletted head. Possibly Monhegan Island, Maine. Ca. 1900. H: 8″; L: 17″. (Blumert-Fiore Collection)

FIG. 207. (RIGHT) *Eider drake*. Anonymous. Wood with polychrome. Maine, Monhegan Island style. Late 19th, early 20th century. L, tail to bill: 14¹/₃″. (Courtesy William Greenspon)

FIG. 208. (BELOW) *Sea gull*. Anonymous. Wood with polychrome, iron rod. Found in Damariscotta, Maine, this "stickup" was carved in two pieces, the head being a variation of inletted construction. Late 19th, early 20th century. L: 13¹/₂″. (Collection of Frank Maresca)

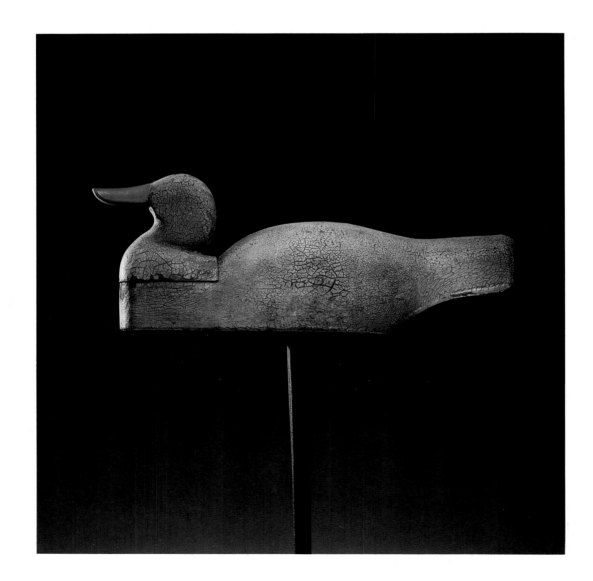

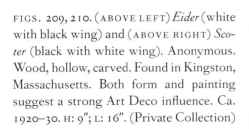

FIGS. 209, 210. (ABOVE LEFT) *Eider* (white with black wing) and (ABOVE RIGHT) *Scoter* (black with white wing). Anonymous. Wood, hollow, carved. Found in Kingston, Massachusetts. Both form and painting suggest a strong Art Deco influence. Ca. 1920–30. H: 9″; L: 16″. (Private Collection)

FIG. 211. (RIGHT) *Working swan decoy.* Anonymous. Laminated construction. Maryland. It is unusual to find a swan decoy depicted with no curves in such a radically geometric fashion. Late 19th, early 20th century. H: 30″; L: 32″. (Private Collection)

FIG. 212. (LEFT) *Crow decoy.* Anonymous. Wood, tin with paint. This stickup was found in Maine and is a rare instance of a decoy with movable wings. The wings flapped when an attached string was pulled. Ca. 1920. L: 14″; w, wingspan: 18″. (Courtesy Edward Thorp Gallery)

FIG. 213. (BELOW) *Gunning or working swan decoy.* From the Orem family, Dorchester County, Maryland. The shooting of swans became illegal early in the 20th century, but swans continued to be used as confidence decoys. Ca. 1880. H: 30″; L: 27″. (The Hall Collection of American Folk and Isolate Art)

FIG. 214. (ABOVE) *Great blue heron*. Anonymous. Hollow body, root neck and head with polychrome. From New Jersey. Two of these herons are known to exist, one with its body in a normal position and this one, with its body inverted. Late 19th century. L, tail to beak: 36″. (The Hall Collection of American Folk and Isolate Art)

FIG. 215. (RIGHT) *Heron decoy*. Anonymous. Laminated wood with polychrome. Found in New Jersey. Ca. 1870–90. H: 22″; L: 28″. (Collection of George Meyer)

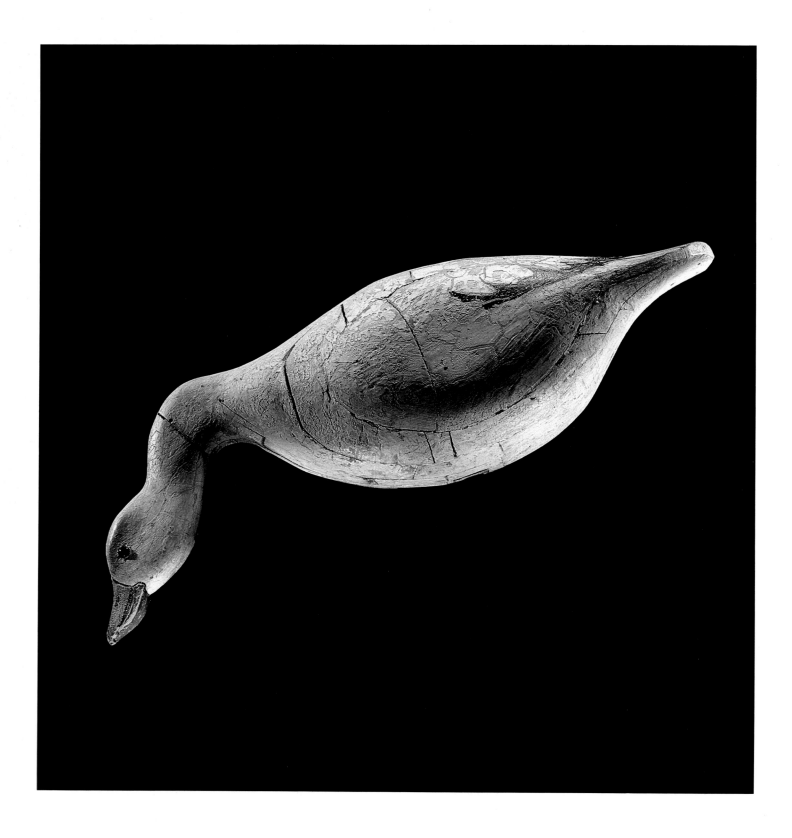

FIG. 216. (OPPOSITE) *Snow goose in feeding position* by John Tax. Osakis, Minnesota. Laminated wood construction with polychrome. L: 26″. (Collection of Mr. and Mrs. Clune Walsh)

FIG. 217. (ABOVE) *Canada goose* by Walter Brady. Oyster, Virginia. Hollow construction, doweled oak bill. This decoy bears a distinct similarity to birds from Cobb Island (see FIG. 222). Ca. 1880. L: 22″. (Private Collection)

FIG. 218. (LEFT) *Yellowlegs* by Tom Wilson. Cedar body, oak bill with polychrome. Wilson (1863–1940), a market hunter who lived in Ipswich, Massachusetts, made decoys for his personal use only. Another example by the same hand is in the collection of the Peabody Museum. Ca. 1890. L: 14″; W: 4″. (Steve Miller Collection)

FIG. 219. (LEFT) *Owl decoy.* Anonymous. Wood, rubber, metal, bottle caps. Found in Winnebago County, Wisconsin. Owls were used as confidence decoys, not to attract other owls but to lure crows. While the crow attacked the owl, the hunter shot the crow. The feather effect was achieved by the sgraffito technique of scratching into the paint while it was wet. Ca. 1920. H: 16¹/₂″. (Private Collection)

FIG. 220. (BELOW LEFT) *Crow decoy.* Anonymous. Cloth saturated with tar over wood frame. Crows were hunted for sport rather than game. This one is constructed like a model airplane. Ca. 1930–40. L: 16″. (Courtesy Cavin-Morris Gallery)

FIG. 221. (BELOW RIGHT) *Crow decoy.* Anonymous. Painted wood. Origin unknown. Ca. 1930–40. L: 16″. (Private Collection)

OPPOSITE:

FIG. 222. (ABOVE LEFT) *Hollow-bodied brant in swimming position* by Nathan Cobb. Wood with polychrome. Cobb Island, Virginia. Ca. 1880. H: 6″; L: 19″. (The Hall Collection of American Folk and Isolate Art)

FIG. 223. (ABOVE RIGHT) *Preening goose.* Anonymous. Traces of paint. Found in Maine although this bird probably originated in the Chesapeake Bay area. Late 19th century. H: 11″; W: 10″; L: 21″. (Private Collection)

FIG. 224. (BELOW LEFT) *Swimming goose stickup decoy.* Anonymous. Wood, traces of paint, extremely weathered. From Maryland. Ca. 1920–30. L: 28″. (Courtesy Ricco-Maresca Gallery)

FIG. 225. (BELOW RIGHT) *Pair of pintail decoys.* Anonymous. Wood with polychrome. Probably of Louisiana origin. Ca. 1930. L, larger: 15¹/₂″; smaller: 9″. (Collection of Michael and Elizabeth Friedman)

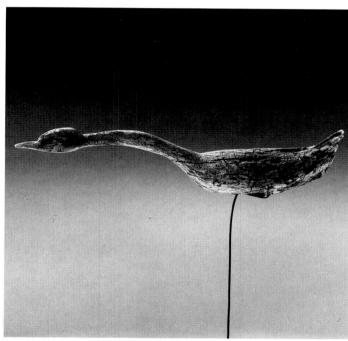

FIG. 226. (LEFT) *Garfish spearing decoy.* Anonymous. Wood with polychrome, metal. From Wisconsin. Ca. 1930–40. L: 10½″. (Collection of George Meyer)

FIG. 227. (BELOW) *Spearing decoy.* Anonymous. Pine with polychrome, metal fins, lead weight. From Minnesota. This colorful decoy resembles an airplane. Ca. 1940–50. L: 12″. (Private Collection)

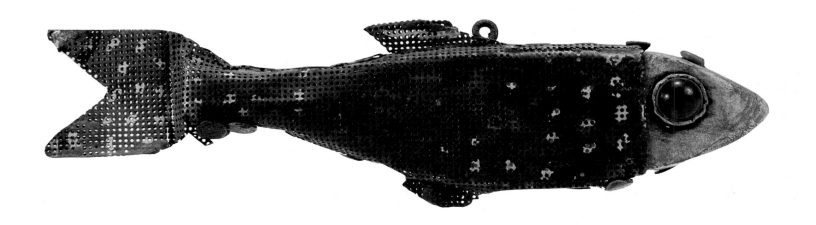

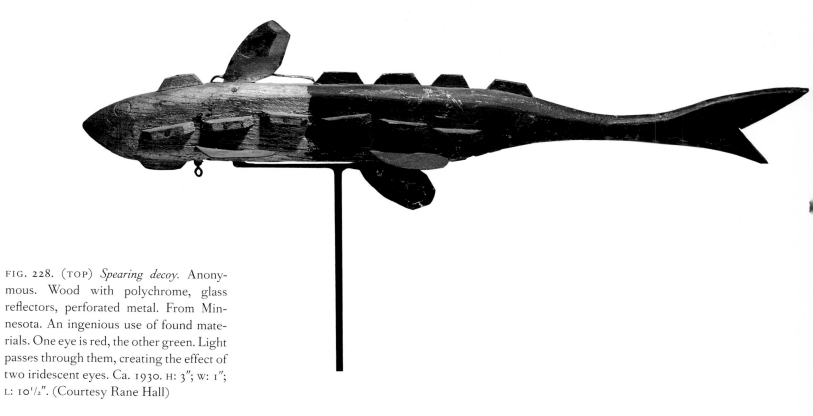

FIG. 228. (TOP) *Spearing decoy.* Anonymous. Wood with polychrome, glass reflectors, perforated metal. From Minnesota. An ingenious use of found materials. One eye is red, the other green. Light passes through them, creating the effect of two iridescent eyes. Ca. 1930. H: 3″; W: 1″; L: 10½″. (Courtesy Rane Hall)

FIG. 229. (ABOVE) *Sturgeon spearing decoy.* Anonymous. Wood with polychrome and tin. From Minnesota. The wood scales are applied. Ca. 1930. L: 21½″. (Courtesy Rane Hall)

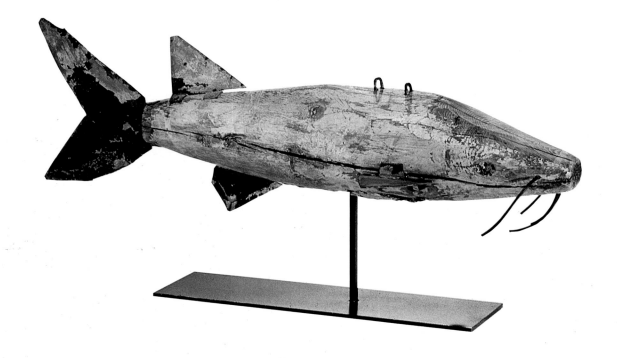

FIG. 230. (ABOVE) *Sturgeon spearing decoy.* Anonymous. Wood with tin fins and tail, rubber barbs, aluminum paint. Found in the Great Lakes area. An extraordinary grace and sense of life has been conveyed with a minimal amount of carving. Ca. 1930–40. L: 24″. (Private Collection)

FIG. 231. (LEFT) *Frog lure.* Anonymous. Horn body with copper fins. Stamped "F" on rear fin. Found in the Northeast. These lures trailed hooks and were used to attract large fish, usually pike. Ca. 1920s. L: 5″. (Collection of Edward Shoffstall)

FIG. 232. (OPPOSITE) *Fish spearing decoy.* Anonymous. Wood, tin and polychrome. This decoy is an extremely long and sleek example. Great Lakes region. Ca. 1940–50. L: 37″. (Private Collection)

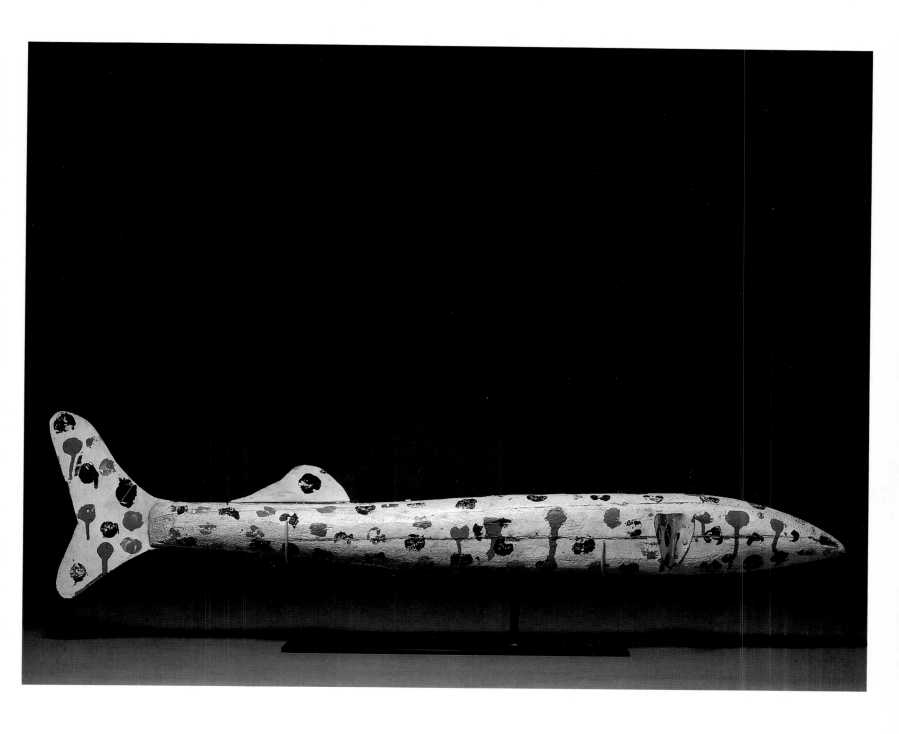

7

CARNIVAL and ENTERTAINMENT

FIG. 233. *Ball-toss board.* Anonymous. Wood with polychrome. Although basically two-dimensional, the relationship of the mouth hole to the painted image gives it a three-dimensional quality. H: 27"; w: 15¾". (Collection of Michael and Elizabeth Friedman)

THE AMERICAN carnival, described by one writer as "cheap, tawdry, not quite honest but still one of the most fascinating of all entertainments,"[11] owed its spread across the nation to hardheaded business considerations. In 1845, the New England traction companies that were building the first electric streetcars had to pay a flat monthly fee rather than a per diem rate for power. Weekday business wasn't enough to make up for slack weekends, so to attract more riders, owners conceived the notion of putting amusement parks at the ends of their lines. These not only featured more or less permanent amusements but also rented space to traveling circuses and carnivals, a concept that expanded as fast as the development of streetcars did.

The history of American carnival life, however, is not found in the business section of libraries but in their music and art divisions. Such histories as there are dwell more on the vividness of the personnel, the hermetic life of the freaks and the trickery in the games of chance than on the art that is an essential part of carnival entertainment. But art there is, and its variety may owe its existence to a carnival philosophy that accounts for its motley forms: "Someone decides," said a carnival owner, "that what

FIG. 234. (LEFT) *Cast-iron shooting gallery target.* Anonymous. This target in the form of a stylized devil's head probably had a bell mounted behind both eyes and the mouth. Found in Pennsylvania. Late 19th century. H: 18″; W: 11″; D: ½″. (Collection of Trotta/ Bono)

the world needs most is a frozen whale and then goes out and gets the whale and freezes it."[12] These sculptures are a testament to that philosophy: each one is the result of a decision on someone's part that it was just what the carnival audience needed to be amused or persuaded to part with its money. A good many of the figures may have been made by the entertainers who used them, like the pedal-animated figure (Fig. 237) and the puppets (Figs. 238 and 244), or were, like the ventriloquist's dummy (Fig. 243), made to order by a person whose trade was producing figures for entertainers.

Carnival and amusement park attractions also used figures that involved a more sophisticated technology than hand carving (Figs. 245, 250, 251 and 252). As expertly crafted as they are, there is no evidence that they were produced in large numbers, and it would seem, from the naiveté of their form and style, that they were commissioned for a specific carnival or amusement facility.

FIG. 235. (OPPOSITE) *Ring-toss figure.* Anonymous. Wood with polychrome. Found in Michigan, this figure had three similar nose-thumbing companions. They were so joined that when an operator pulled a cord, the figures would pivot left and right, becoming moving targets challenging the ring tosser's skill. Early 20th century. H: 32″. (Private Collection)

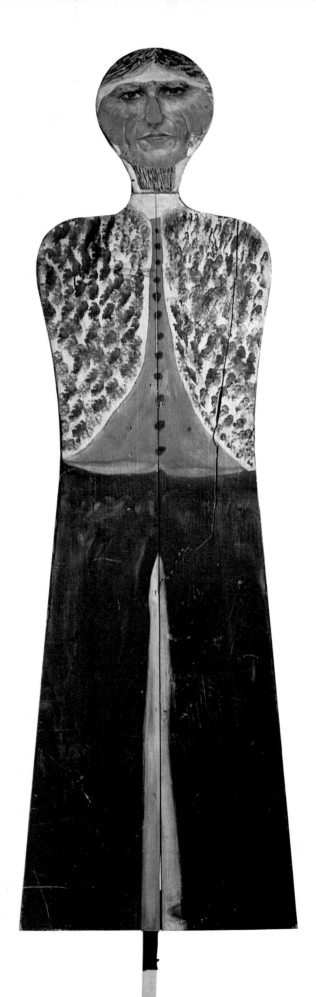

FIG. 236. (OPPOSITE) *Ball-toss target.* Anonymous. Wood with polychrome. Found in New England. The chromolithographed face was a commercially produced toy mask, a "penny mask." In this case it was attached by a hinge and would snap back when struck with a ball. Ca. 1920–40. H: 60″. (Collection of Jack and Ali Clift)

While carnival sideshows tested credulity, carnival games of chance challenged skill, sometimes in the form of a taunt, like the ring-toss figure (Fig. 235) that insultingly thumbed its nose or the figure (Fig. 242) that squirted water from its mouth when the target was missed.

Since much carnival sculpture was created more as tools of carnival trade than as art, few of the artists are known, but one entertainer, an amateur who created amusements for his own and his family's and neighbors' entertainment, received a certain amount of local fame. He was J. Wallace Brungart, who early in his youth learned both cabinetmaking and machinist skills and later in life spent most of his free time making working models of turn-of-the-century Americana. He used homemade machinery contrived from parts of an old treadle machine, and for the works themselves he used wood from razed landmarks. He refused to sell any of his pieces, and donated some of them to the Hershey Museum in Pennsylvania.

The difference between Brungart's imaginative amusement figures and those of a real carnival is that his were made simply as a matter of self-expression, a hobby; carnival sculptures are the product of necessity. Yet in both instances, the results have been works of considerable significance.

FIG. 237. (RIGHT) *Seated man.* Wood with polychrome, fabric, buttons. The legend "Howard Yellis, Farmersville-Easton 3, PH Stocker No. 265-11" is stamped on the back of this elegantly dressed figure. It was discovered in a Philadelphia flea market and may have been one of a number of figures used in a minstrel show. Foot pedals located behind the chair were used to animate it. Early 20th century. H: 33″. (Collection of Allan and Ellen Cober)

FIG. 238. (LEFT) *Minstrel puppets*. Anonymous. Wood with polychrome and fabric. These puppets were once dressed and animated by a mechanism in a cigar box. On the scale of minstrel figures represented, these are the most elementary in construction. Early 20th century. H: 26″ and 29″. (Private Collection)

FIG. 239. (BELOW) *Calliope figure*. Anonymous. Wood with polychrome, fabric, leather. This figure is a primitive interpretation of the more formal figures produced by the Hirschal-Spillman Carousel Co. in Tonawanda, New York. They were used on the carousel to create the illusion that the figure was working the pipe organ. Late 19th, early 20th century. H: 48″. (Collection of Allan and Ellen Cober)

FIG. 240. (LEFT) *Ventriloquist's dummy head.* Anonymous. Composition material with polychrome, string, fabric. Found in Pennsylvania. Late 19th century. H: 6″. (Blumert-Fiore Collection)

FIG. 241. (BELOW) *Ventriloquist's dummy head.* Anonymous. Wood with polychrome. Origin unknown. Late 19th century. H: 9¾″. (Private Collection)

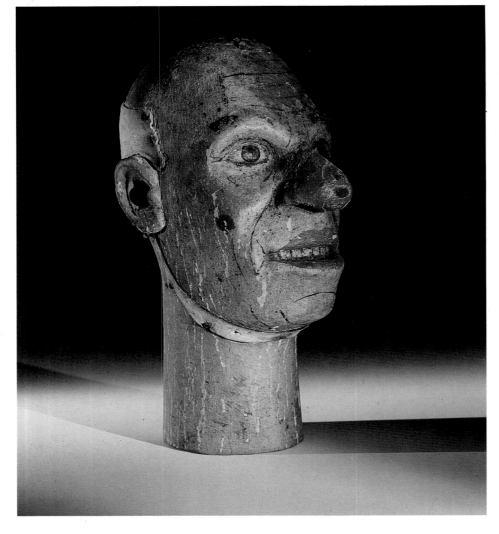

FIG. 242. (LEFT) *Carnival head.* Anonymous. Wood with polychrome, leather. This was made with a tube through which it would squirt water from its mouth. Ca. 1920–30. H: 9″. (Collection of Helen and Scudder Smith)

FIG. 243. (ABOVE) *Ventriloquist's dummy head.* Anonymous. Wood with traces of paint. Found in New England. Late 19th, early 20th century. H: 8″. (Private Collection)

FIG. 244. (OPPOSITE) *Puppet.* Anonymous. Wood with polychrome, fabric. Southern origin. Late 19th century. H: 23³⁄₄″. (Private Collection)

FIG. 245. (LEFT) *Ventriloquist's dummy head.* Anonymous. Mixed metals with polychrome. Found on Long Island, New York. Dummy heads were rarely made of metal. The brass eyes of this one roll up and back, the tongue protrudes when the mouth opens, and it once had tubes inside through which it could blow smoke through its nose. Mid to late 19th century. H: 8½". (Courtesy William Greenspon)

FIG. 246. (BELOW) *Hand puppet.* Anonymous. Pine. Found in New England. Late 19th century. H: 8"; W: 4". (Private Collection)

FIG. 247. (RIGHT) *Man and wife puppets* by J. Wallace Brungart. Wood with polychrome, fabric, animal hair, fur. Brungart (1877–1968) lived in Glen Rock, Pennsylvania, and worked in his basement producing hundreds of carvings: animals, puppets, miniature furniture and tiny models of farm machinery. These figures appear to represent an Amish couple. Dated July 5, 1950. H, man: 25½"; woman: 25". (Collection of Gary and Cheryl Heimbuch)

FIG. 248. (RIGHT) *Devil puppet heads* by J. Wallace Brungart. Wood with polychrome, animal hair and fur, wire, tin. These were undoubtedly part of Brungart's local puppet shows. Dated June 1950. H, larger head: 10½"; smaller: 6¼". (Collection of Gary and Cheryl Heimbuch)

FIG. 249. (LEFT) *Ventriloquist's dummy torso.* Anonymous. Wood with polychrome, hair, canvas. This piece was once clothed and used in a tent show known as the Dawson Comedy Company, located in Canton, Ohio. As with many of these dummies, the pole, visible in the opening, operated the head. Ca. 1860. H: 25″; W: 13″; D: 7″. (Private Collection)

FIGS. 250, 251. (OPPOSITE) *Baseball catcher and batter.* Anonymous. Brass, iron, white metal. Found in Saratoga, New York, these concession figures were once clothed and electrically automated; the catcher moved his mitt up and down, and when the plate in his mitt was struck, the mitt closed, the eyes lit up, and smoke emerged from his nose and mouth. The other figure, which once held a bat, worked the same way. Although patented as of October 12, 1925, there is no indication that they ever went into manufacture. H: 61″. (Courtesy William Greenspon)

FIG. 252. (LEFT) *Boxing figure.* Anonymous. Painted rubber and fabric. The conception, design and manufacture of figures of this type probably involved the ingenuity and talents of several local people to produce a carnival game of skill. An inner mechanism controlled by a hand lever caused the arms of the figure to make jabbing and punching motions. Ca. 1930–40. H: 24³/₄″. (Private Collection)

FIG. 253. (OPPOSITE) *Gorilla.* Laminated and carved wood with polychrome. Believed to have been part of the fun house at the Coney Island amusement park. Though probably carved in a shop, the figure exhibits strong individual stylization. Late 19th, early 20th century. H: 29″ top of head to bottom of base; W: 18″; D: 12″. (Private Collection)

8

CANES

MORE OFTEN than not, canes are thought of as walking sticks for the elderly and disabled or as fashion accessories. Yet through the centuries, in both nonindustrial and Western societies, they have been made into art objects by means of carving or embellishment. Some of the finest examples are to be found among American hand-carved canes made when something other than need motivated their creation. Like a staff or a scepter, a carved cane is a highly personal object, and as such tends to confirm the identity or the status, real or wished for, of its owner. It is not likely, then, that the sculpted canes shown here were used simply as support for infirm legs.

Walking sticks were and still are a cultural tradition among Southern Afro-Americans, and many, because they are characterized by reptilian and animal motifs (Figs. 276 and 278) are reminiscent of African ritual sculptures, in which such themes occur with frequency. Canes so carved are sometimes known as "conjure sticks," and were often made by or for root doctors and local healers. Other Southern canes with heads or figures (Figs. 259 and 273) are, because of their strong similarity to African sculpture, also thought to be Afro-American.

Cane carving is a whittler's art; its basic material—usually a sturdy branch—is easily available, easy to hold and easy to carve, compared with the more ambitious freestanding figure. Too, it lends itself to the whiling away of leisure hours in a fanciful occupation that results in imaginative sculpture. Often the shape of a root (Fig. 280) or a fallen tree limb has activated a cane carver's hand and fantasy, but in the case of the maker of one intricately carved and lavishly detailed cane (Fig. 282), it may have been personal participation in the Civil War that urged him to create a memorial to it.

Perhaps because of the bulbous shape of branch ends, heads are a favorite subject for knobs, but canes with erotic handles (Figs. 267 and 273) are both rare and striking.

Since canes, more than most other works of art, are easily transportable, and can be begun in one place and finished in another, they often show the influence of contact with other cultures. The ones in Figs. 254 and 255, inasmuch as they exhibit some stylistic resemblance to the work of Oceanic peoples, were probably carved by sailors, whereas Fig. 257 strongly resembles wood carvings made on Easter Island.

Most art can be viewed and appreciated from some reasonable distance; canes, on the other hand, being small in size, must be held in one's hand to study and savor their artistry. Then one discovers that cane sculpture, though diminutive, displays, when successful, the same strength, power, mystery and design as any other sculptural work presented in this book.

FIG. 256. (LEFT) *Staff with head.* Anonymous. Carved from one piece of wood, it was found in South Carolina. The head has a hole in the top which may have held a candle. Detail: 15″; total length: 48″. (Private Collection)

FIG. 257. (ABOVE) *Cane, man with goatee.* Anonymous. Wood, traces of paint, taxidermist's glass eyes. Origin unknown. It is thought to be a captain's going-ashore cane. Late 19th century. Detail: 8″; total length: 35″. (Brian Collection)

FIG. 258. (LEFT) *Cane, claw and head.* Anonymous. Wood, bead eyes, metal finial. This is a rather grimly amusing variation of the "ball and claw" construction found in furniture legs. Late 19th century. Detail: 4½″; total length: 34¾″. (Collection of George Meyer)

FIG. 259. (ABOVE LEFT) *Cane with man's head.* Hardwood, varnish. This cane was bought from a black family in South Carolina. It is initialed "J.C.H." and shows a strong similarity to the carvings of the Yoruba people of West Africa. Mid-19th century. Detail: 6"; total length: 35". (Collection of Timothy and Pamela Hill)

FIG. 260. (ABOVE RIGHT) *Cane with man's head.* Anonymous. Wood, traces of paint. The eyes are glass beads and there is a snake carved on the staff. Probably of Southern origin. Late 19th, early 20th century. Detail: 3"; total length: 36". (Collection of George Meyer)

FIG. 261. (RIGHT) *Cane with man's head.* Anonymous. Maple, traces of paint, metal flange. Snakes entwined on the staff. Found in New England. Early 20th century. Detail: 5"; total length: 36". (Collection of Timothy and Pamela Hill)

FIG. 262. (RIGHT) *Cane.* Anonymous. Maple branch with polychrome. Found in Moorestown, New Jersey. Ca. 1870–90. Detail: 2½″; total length: 32″. (Blumert-Fiore Collection)

FIG. 263. (BELOW) *Walking stick with seated figure.* Anonymous. Sequoia wood, painted, coral bead eyes, metal button. From California. This hollow walking stick is made of four pieces of laminated wood with undulations down the entire staff. Early 20th century. Detail: 6″; total length: 33″. (Collection of George Meyer)

FIG. 264. (BELOW RIGHT) *Cane with head in hand.* Wood, varnish. The name "Frank H. Morgan" is carved on the staff. Late 19th century. Detail: 6″; head: 2″; total length: 36″. (Collection of George Meyer)

FIG. 265. (BELOW) *Cane with two faces.* Anonymous. Walnut. Found in New York State. The handle is attached with a screw. Ca. 1900. Detail: 7″; total length: 35″. (Collection of Timothy and Pamela Hill)

FIG. 266. (OPPOSITE) *Cane with bathing beauty.* Anonymous. Pine with polychrome. From South Carolina. Ca. 1920s. Detail: 12½″; total length: 34½″. (Collection of Timothy and Pamela Hill)

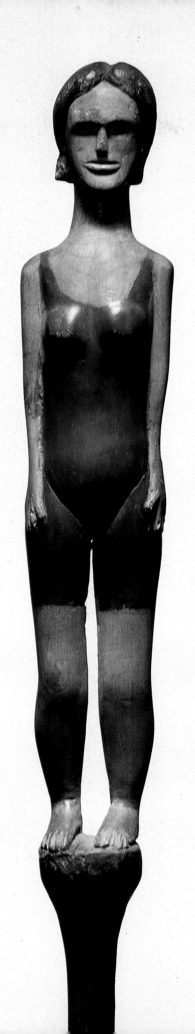

FIG. 267. (OPPOSITE) *Cane with woman devoured by animals* by Denzil Goodpasture. Kentucky. Polychromed wood, glass eyes. Goodpasture's canes are lavishly painted, usually depict animals and often include women. Recently, he has ventured into portraiture canes, such as one modeled after Dolly Parton. Ca. 1981–82. Detail: 6″; total length: 35″. (Herbert Waide Hemphill, Jr., Collection)

FIG. 268. (RIGHT) *Cane with nude woman.* Anonymous. Walnut. Found in New York and carved in the manner of a ship's figurehead, this cane is thought to be the work of a sailor. Late 19th century. Detail: 6″; total length: 34¹/₂″. (Collection of George Meyer)

FIG. 269. (BELOW) *Erotic cane.* Anonymous. Wood. The face of the figure is Oriental. That and the bird tattoo incised on the back shoulder suggest it may have been made by a sailor. Late 19th century. Detail: 4″; total length: 32″. (Collection of Timothy and Pamela Hill)

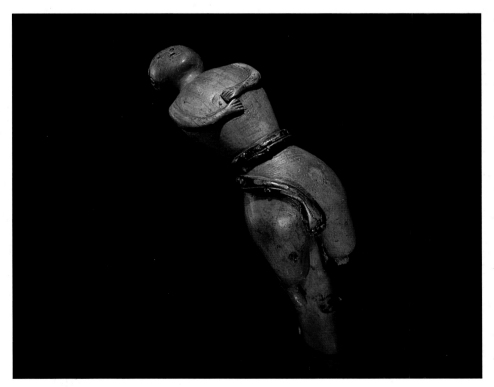

FIG. 270. (LEFT) *Whimsy cane.* Anonymous. Walnut. Found in New England. This delicate cane is carved from one piece of wood. The balls and chain move freely within the construction. Late 19th century. Total length: 36″. (Collection of Timothy and Pamela Hill)

FIG. 271. (BELOW) *Cane with reclining nude.* Anonymous. Wood with polychrome. Found in New York State. Ca. 1930. Detail: 9½″; total length: 36″. (Collection of George Meyer)

FIG. 272. (OPPOSITE) *Cane with Janus figures, woman and man.* Anonymous. Wood, yellow paint. Found in Athens, Georgia. Mid-19th century. Detail: 8½″; total length: 35″. (Collection of George Meyer)

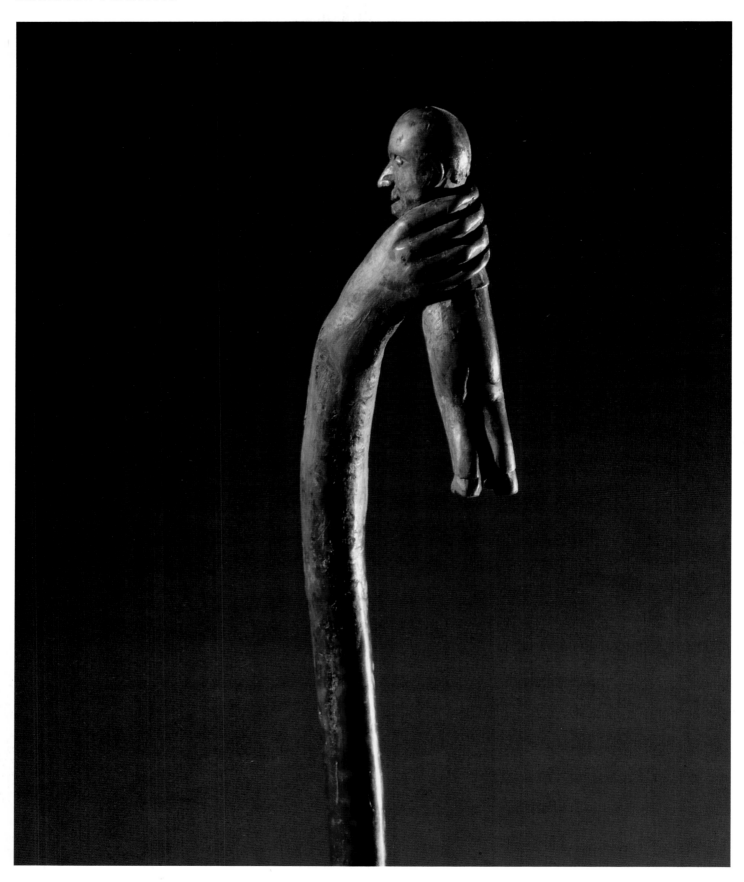

FIG. 274. (LEFT) *Cane with man with heart in hand.* Anonymous. Carved from a tree branch containing a burl. The natural form suggested the head as well as the heart coming out of the hand. The eyes are pebbles. Early 20th century. Detail: 7¹/₂″; total length: 36″. (Collection of George Meyer)

FIG. 275. (BELOW) *Cane with crouching man.* Anonymous. Pine, copper flange. Early 20th century. Detail: 6″; total length: 36″. (Collection of Timothy and Pamela Hill)

FIG. 273. (OPPOSITE) *Cane with man seized in a grip.* Anonymous. Wood with varnish. Origin unknown. When turned upside down, the shape of the original branch becomes evident. Late 19th century. Detail: 3¹/₂″. (Private Collection)

FIG. 276. (LEFT) *Snake cane.* Anonymous. Maple, traces of paint. Early 20th century. Total length: 33″. (Herbert Waide Hemphill, Jr., Collection)

FIG. 277. (BELOW AND DETAIL BELOW LEFT) *Cane with man's head caught in snake coils.* Anonymous. Ash with polychrome. Midwest origin. The tiny hand carved at the end of the cane handle holds a finely detailed ear of corn. Ca. 1900. Total length: 37″. (Collection of Timothy and Pamela Hill)

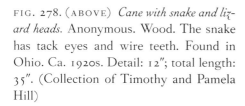

FIG. 278. (ABOVE) *Cane with snake and lizard heads.* Anonymous. Wood. The snake has tack eyes and wire teeth. Found in Ohio. Ca. 1920s. Detail: 12″; total length: 35″. (Collection of Timothy and Pamela Hill)

FIG. 279. (ABOVE RIGHT) *Cane with dog head handle.* Anonymous. Walnut, traces of paint, glass jewel eyes. Found in Tennessee. Ca. 1910. Detail: 8½″; total length: 36″. (Collection of Timothy and Pamela Hill)

FIG. 280. (RIGHT) *Cane with "root" deer head handle.* Anonymous. Maple, varnish, black paint. Found in Maine. The root formation was so suggestive it required only minimal carving to accent its resemblance to a deer. Late 19th century. Detail: 9″; total length: 39″. (Blumert-Fiore Collection)

FIG. 281. (OPPOSITE) *Cane, Venus form.* Anonymous. Maple, varnish. Found in Ohio. The natural shape of the root required only the trimming of the roots that form the arms and legs and the most minimal amount of carving on the face. Late 19th century. Detail: 6½″; total length: 35″. (Blumert-Fiore Collection)

FIG. 282. (RIGHT) *Commemoration cane.* Anonymous. Wood with varnish, pewter knob. This finely carved cane shows a soldier carrying a flag, horse and rider, and calligraphy commemorating Civil War battle sites and the Second Battalion, Fourth Ohio Volunteer Cavalry. Ca. 1865–70. Total length: 33½″. (Collection of George Meyer)

9

ANIMALS

WHEN FIRST paint was put to a flat surface, chisel to stone, knife to wood, animals of every kind were subjects for art and artists all over the world. However, in American primitive and naive sculptural works, there are particularly surprising concepts and adventurous uses of unconventional materials.

Animals as toys are common enough, but an oversized pull-toy hippo (Fig. 330) assembled out of bottle caps is an arresting example of the use of unexpected materials for sculpture as well as a remarkable exercise in pure fantasy. (The maker of that toy evidently had an enormous collection of caps, for he is known to have made a bottle-cap giraffe as well.)

Artists have been moved to memorialize a beloved pet and companion (Fig. 305) or to portray certain animals as symbols of strength, like the lion head serving as a capital (Fig. 329) for the mantelpiece of an Adirondacks hunting lodge, or of power and sharp vision in the form of a pilothouse eagle (Fig. 316) which once perched on the highest point of a Maine coastal ship.

Rocking horses especially, though designed as toys, are examples of form following function, which resulted in an extraordinary diversity of

FIG. 283. *Peacock.* Anonymous. The body of this ingenious and humorous assemblage is composed of laminated sections of wood, its neck and tail are sections of furniture legs that have been minimally carved and the beak and legs are piano stool legs. The comb is a fragment of a Victorian hinge. Early 20th century. H: 27″; L: 34″. (Private Collection)

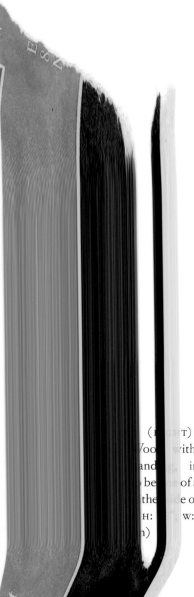

FIG. 284. (OPPOSITE) *Snake gate.* Anonymous. Wrought iron. These snakes were bolted to a farm gate in upstate New York. Late 19th, early 20th century. H: 32″; W: 15½″. (Private Collection)

(RIGHT) *Horse head.* Anonymous. Wood with polychrome, sheet-and iron brace supports. be of a pair said to have been the of a stable entrance. Ca. H: W: 15″; D: 1½″. (Private)

sculptural stylization (Figs. 295, 297 and 300). Animals become trade signs or architectural embellishments, as did the pigeon head (Fig. 313) from the Pigeon Cove Inn and the raven that stood atop a hunting lodge in Maine (Fig. 315). Too, there are beautiful examples of utilitarian sculpture: wood snakes (Figs. 323 and 324), though often intended to be put in barns to scare off rodents, are exquisite works.

Of particular elegance are pieces sculpted of whale ivory, the material of the sailor scrimshander. It is a medium that invites and takes extremely fine detail and retains its structural strength even when carved with a latticework design. This fact, coupled with the carver's infinite patience and need for diversion on long voyages, has made for the creation of extremely graceful and delicate carvings, many of which depicted animals of both sea and land (Figs. 320, 321 and 322). These images were often cleverly integrated into a utilitarian object, like a fork or pie-dough crimper, meant as a gift to someone back home.

There is, of course, art for art's sake. Raymond Coins, a twentieth-century artist, says his work (Fig. 307) comes out of his dreams, while the peacock made of found objects (Fig. 283) is simply the work of someone with a sense of humor as well as art. Often works like these are created simply because the sculptor felt like making them, a not unusual reason for creating art, and the choice of subject is a consequence of a reason no more complex than that the sculptor wanted to make that particular animal at that particular time.

FIG. 286. (RIGHT) *Owl* by Albert Zahn. Baileys Harbor, Wisconsin. Wood with polychrome. Zahn was a prolific carver. Much of his work was religiously inspired and often depicted simple geometric stylizations of people and animals. Ca. 1935–40. H: 14″; W: 5″; D: 5″. (Private Collection; photo courtesy Ricco-Johnson Gallery)

FIG. 287. (BELOW) *Child's horse toy*. Anonymous. Oxidized wood, horsehair tail and decorative cloth band. The four legs are each attached with nails to the flat body. A separate wood post may have terminated in a wheeled base or possibly was held in a child's hand for play. Found in Maine. Late 19th, early 20th century. H: 16″; L: 22″. (Private Collection)

FIG. 288. (OPPOSITE) *Peacock on a book*. Anonymous. Wood with polychrome, fiber pompons. Found in Maine, this is one of two almost identical carvings. Ca. 1840–50. H: 16″; L: 27″. (Private Collection)

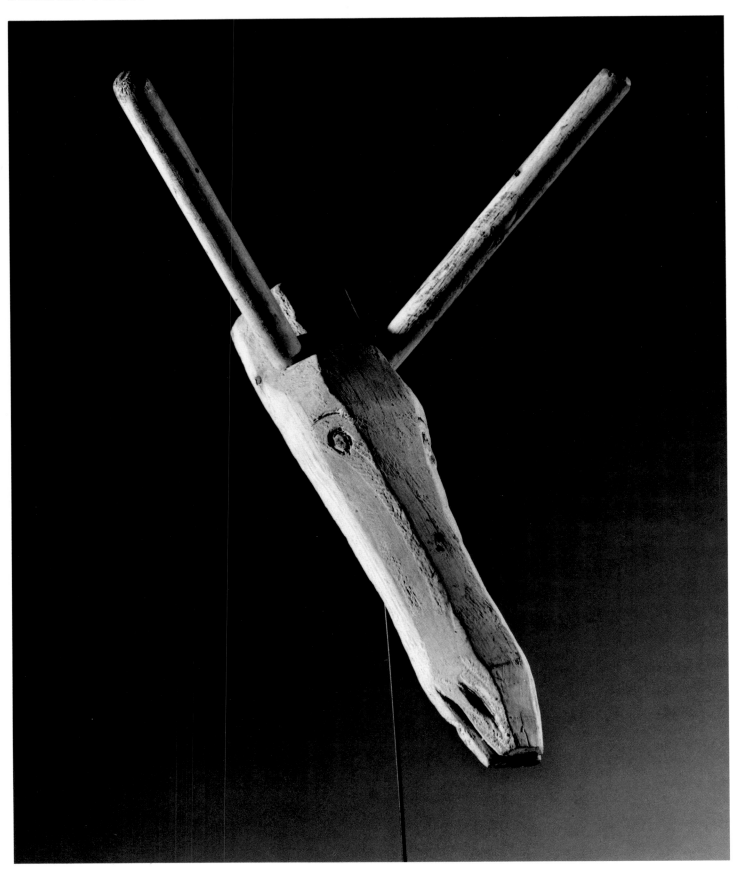

FIG. 289. (OPPOSITE) *Steer head tack rack.* Anonymous. Pine with polychrome. This head once held riding gear in a horse barn in Texas. Early 20th century. H: 15″; w, at horns: 12″. (Private Collection)

FIG. 290. (ABOVE) *Prancing horse.* Anonymous. Made out of found and minimally shaped roots and branches. The surface has been covered with tar and paint. Early 20th century. H: 25½″; L: 29″. (Private Collection)

FIG. 291. (CENTER) *Horse with white fetlocks.* Wood with polychrome, horsehair, iron horseshoes. Once a fixture in a window of a saddle shop. Late 19th, early 20th century. H: 32″; L: 35″. (Collection of Larry and Gloria Silverstein)

FIG. 292. (RIGHT) *Jumping carousel horse.* Anonymous. Pine with polychrome, iron bracing. Found in Maryland. The majority of carousel animals were shop made and had a more formal character than this one, which, not shop produced, was probably used in a country carousel. Late 19th century. L: 49″. (Collection of Frederick B. Hanson)

FIG. 293. (LEFT) *Horse toy.* Anonymous. Wood, black paint, braided horsehair, tack eyes. Late 19th, early 20th century. H: 15″; L: 20″. (Private Collection)

FIG. 294. (BELOW LEFT) *Horse.* Anonymous. Wood with varnish. Found in New England. Late 19th century. H: 8¹/₂″; W: 2¹/₂″; L: 8¹/₂″. (Private Collection)

FIG. 295. (BELOW RIGHT) *Rocking horse.* Anonymous. Wood with polychrome, horsehair. Found in Schenectady, New York. Second half 19th century. H: 30″; W: 10″; L: 46″. (Courtesy Aarne Anton American Primitive Gallery)

FIG. 296. (OPPOSITE) *Torso of horse.* Anonymous. Wood with polychrome. Although the four legs are missing, the wear in the area of the painted saddle indicates it was probably used as a child's toy. Found in upstate New York. Late 19th century. H: 15″; W: 3″; L: 27″. (Collection of the Ricco-Maresca Gallery)

FIG. 297. (ABOVE) *Spotted rocking horse.* Anonymous. Wood with polychrome. Origin unknown. Late 19th century. H: 29″; L: 53″. (Private Collection)

FIG. 298. (OPPOSITE) *Pair of horses.* Anonymous. Wood, paint, horsehair. The form of these horses is evocative of the style of horse carving often seen on American Indian catlinite pipes. Late 19th century. H: 10⅞″; L: 14½″. (Private Collection)

FIG. 299. (OPPOSITE) *Rocking horse* (rockers missing). Anonymous. Wood, leather saddle with polychrome. 19th century. H: 24″; L: 41″. (Private Collection)

FIG. 300. (ABOVE) *Rocking horse chair.* Anonymous. Walnut and pine. Found in Pennsylvania. Ca. 1870. H: 21″; L: 36″; W: 14″. (Collection of Maggie and Jessie Hill)

FIG. 301. (RIGHT) *Horse.* Anonymous. Weathered wood. Weathering has changed this toy, emphasizing the simplicity and elegance of its form. Late 19th century. H: 15½″; L: 12½″. (Private Collection)

FIG. 302. (ABOVE) *Woodland scene.* Anonymous. Wood with polychrome. Found in Pennsylvania. Early 20th century. H: 18″; W: 24¹/₂″; D: 1³/₄″. (Collection of George Meyer)

FIG. 303. (LEFT) *Man and a poodle* by Wilhelm Schimmel. Wood with polychrome. Schimmel, born in 1817 in Hesse-Darmstadt, Germany, an immigrant itinerant worker and irascible alcoholic, died in a Pennsylvania poorhouse in August 1890, leaving behind what has become an important legacy of carvings. He seldom did human figures. H: 4¹/₂″; L: 7″. (Private Collection)

FIG. 304. (RIGHT) *Polar bear*. Anonymous. Pine with polychrome. Found in Maine. 20th century. H: 13½″; W: 11¾″; L: 29″. (Private Collection)

FIG. 305. (BELOW) *Spotted dog* by Edgar Tolson. Kentucky. Stone. This is one of eight stone carvings by Tolson (1904–84), who usually carved or whittled his works in wood. H: 30″; W: 15″; L: 23″. (The Hall Collection of American Folk and Isolate Art)

FIG. 308. (OPPOSITE) *Lion.* Anonymous. Brownstone. The highly skillful carving and naive proportions of this piece suggest it was made by a stone tradesman. Since its creation, it remained in Rutherford, New Jersey, and was only recently removed. Ca. 1875–90. H: 22″; L: 41″; W: 18″. (Courtesy Ricco-Maresca Gallery)

FIG. 306. (ABOVE) *Resting dog.* Anonymous. Sandstone. This carved stone dog was one of a pair flanking a building entryway. Found in Ohio. Early 20th century. H: 17″; L: 27″. (Private Collection)

FIG. 307. (RIGHT) *Stone sheep* by Raymond Coins, North Carolina. Ca. 1980. H: 10³/₄″; L: 15¹/₂″; D: 4″. (Courtesy Ricco-Maresca Gallery)

FIG. 309. (LEFT) *Bird tree.* Anonymous. Wood with polychrome, forged steel. Birds and bird trees in every medium are ubiquitous in Pennsylvania folk art, probably because of their symbolic meaning in religion. Ca. 1800. H: 24″; w, at widest point: 11½″. (Courtesy Robert E. Kinnaman and Brian A. Ramakers)

FIG. 310. (OPPOSITE) *Bird of prey in flight.* Anonymous. Wood with polychrome. From Dover, Delaware. This elegantly carved bird is difficult to identify, but seems to be a bird of prey. Late 19th century. L: 16″; w: 28″. (Courtesy Frederick B. Hanson; Private Collection)

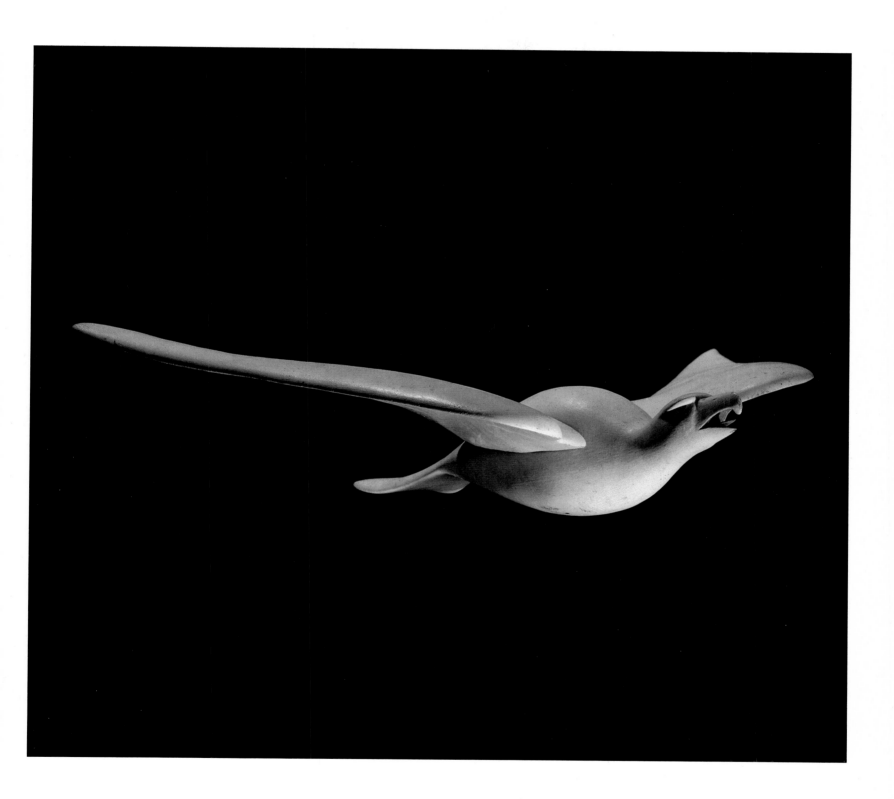

FIG. 311. (LEFT) *Pair of bird finials.* Anonymous. Wood with varnish. Found in New England. Late 19th century. H: 3¼″; W: 2¾″; L: 5¼″. (Private Collection)

FIG. 312. (BELOW) *Rooster with a top hat.* Anonymous. Wood with paint. Found in Pennsylvania, this carving may have been used as a trade sign. Late 19th, early 20th century. H: 14″; W: 20″. (Private Collection)

FIG. 313. (OPPOSITE) *Pigeon head.* Anonymous. Wood with polychrome. A total of three pigeon heads, all hollow, were mounted around the perimeter of the Pigeon Cove Inn, in Nob, Maine. Early 19th century. H: 20″; W: 20″; L: 25″. (Collection of Helen and Scudder Smith)

FIG. 314. (OPPOSITE) *Snow owl.* Anonymous. White cedar with polychrome. Found in New England. Ca. 1920. H: 21″; W: 7″. (Steve Miller Collection)

FIG. 315. (ABOVE) *Raven.* Anonymous. Wood, black paint, cast metal legs. This large bird was once attached to the roof of a hunting lodge in Maine. Ca. 1920–30. H: 27″; L, tail to beak: 44″. (Brian Collection)

FIG. 316. (RIGHT) *Eagle perched on a stone.* Anonymous. Pine with polychrome. This pilothouse eagle at one time graced a Maine coastal ship. Ca. 1875. H: 31″; W: 58″; D: 22″. (Collection of William Greenspon)

FIG. 317. (LEFT) *Owl.* H: 18″; W: 5″. (Collection of Patricia Guthman)

FIG. 318. (BELOW) *Eagle perched on a book.* H: 17½″; W: 10″; D: 5½″. (Collection of Patricia Guthman)

FIG. 319. (OPPOSITE) *Tortoise.* L, head to tail: 12″; W: 9″; D: 2½″. (Collection of Patricia Guthman)

The anonymous carver, said to be from New Hampshire, left an extensive body of work, most of which represented different species of birds. They were all of wood, either painted or polychromed. Late 19th, early 20th century.

FIG. 320. (RIGHT) *Running dog pie crimper.*
Anonymous. Whale ivory and baleen. A
particularly fine example of a familiar motif
in scrimshaw work. Mid-19th century. L:
7¹⁄₈″. (Collection of Howard and Catherine
Feldman)

FIG. 321. (LEFT) *Sea horse pie crimper.* Anonymous. Whale ivory. 19th century. H: 2″; L: 6″. (Collection of Howard and Catherine Feldman)

FIG. 322. (BELOW) *Snake pie crimper.* Anonymous. Whale ivory and baleen. 19th century. L: 6″. (Collection of Howard and Catherine Feldman)

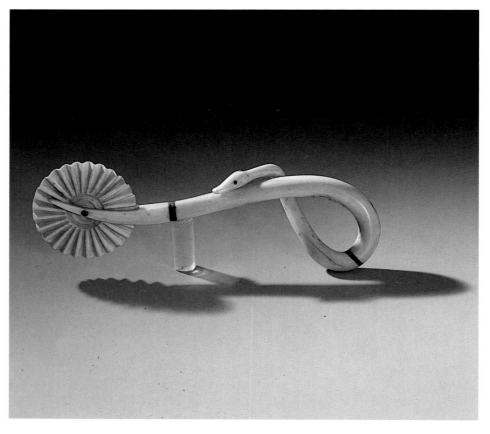

FIG. 323. (RIGHT) *Tiger maple snake.* Anonymous. Maple with varnish. This snake, though obviously made from a branch, has been carved to suggest a snake in motion. The tiger dappling of the maple gives the illusion of snakeskin. Root snake carvings were often used in a barn for the purpose of frightening rodents. Late 19th, early 20th century. L: 32″. (Marvel Collection)

FIG. 324. (BELOW) *Root snake.* Anonymous. Wood with polychrome. Origin unknown. Early 20th century. W, coil: 10″. (Collection of Helen and Scudder Smith)

FIG. 325. (RIGHT) *Slingshot.* Anonymous. Wood with polychrome. Found in Texas. A common toy, simple, but with strong graphic impact and carved out of a bit of tree branch. Ca. 1920–30. H: 7¹/₂″. (Private Collection)

FIG. 326. (BELOW) *Staff of intertwined snakes.* Anonymous. Forged iron. The finial on top is an herb leaf. This seems to be a variation of a caduceus and may have been a doctor's office sign or a pharmacy ornament. Late 19th century. H: 22″. (Brian Collection)

FIG. 327. (OPPOSITE ABOVE) *Dog pursuing a deer.* Anonymous. Pine with polychrome. This is all that remains of a once large whirligig. First quarter 19th century. H: 8″; L: 36″. (Private Collection)

FIG. 328. (OPPOSITE) *Fish plaque* by Oscar Peterson. Michigan. Wood with polychrome. Peterson (1887–1951), a handyman, earned a good part of his income carving, painting and selling fish decoys. His plaques and three-dimensional works were done as gifts. This one hung in a bar in Cadillac, Michigan. Ca. 1930. H: 9³/₄″; W: 28³/₄″. (Collection of Michael Garden)

FIG. 329. (ABOVE) *Lion head.* Anonymous. Pine with polychrome. This stylized lion head was used as a capital for a mantelpiece of a fireplace in an upstate New York lodge. Late 19th, early 20th century. H: 10¹/₂″; W: 15″; D: 15″. (Private Collection)

FIG. 330. (OPPOSITE) *Hippopotamus pull toy.* Anonymous. Wood, bottle caps with polychrome. When the hippo is pulled, his mouth opens and closes. This hippo and a similarly constructed giraffe were found in Maine. Bottle-cap sculptures have been turning up since metal bottle caps came into common use. Ca. 1968. H: 42″; L: 50″. (Herbert Waide Hemphill, Jr., Collection)

10

IDIOSYNCRATIC
and OUTSIDER ART

FIG. 331. *Assemblage*. Wood, metal. This piece, although it looks functional, isn't. It was made over the course of several years by a man in confinement in Newbern, Vermont. Ca. 1880. H: 60″; W: 48″. (Collection of Kenneth and Ida Manko)

NAIVE AND amateur artists as a group, painters and sculptors alike, particularly those of the previous two centuries and the first half of the twentieth, tended to produce works that echoed the academic art traditions of their times. However fresh and unusual the results of their efforts, most very likely were striving to emulate either reality or "fine" art. Often the intention was use rather than aesthetics, or, to put it another way, to make something intended for use aesthetically pleasing.

Mass manufacture has nearly eliminated the economic incentive for handcraft, and reduced working hours, especially since World War II, have made possible increased leisure time. As a consequence, in latter-day naive sculpture, much if not most of the work is primarily art for art's sake. The artists don't necessarily have any ambition to be artists in the formal sense of the word, but are impelled for one reason or another to "make" art. While the majority of these artists still attempt to approximate academic reality, there are within this general category of artists a group who display total independence of vision, whose art is self-determined, or, as Joanna Cubbs put it, "self-generated,"[13] and the form it takes is unconnected to cultural influences or consciousness of art movements and essentially has no roots in any art tradition.

The work of these contemporary naives tends to have much more a quality of abandon than does the main body of naive and primitive art. Color is used with a free hand and with little regard for its aptness to the three-dimensional form the color lies upon, and often the application of color seems to conflict with or violate the silhouette of the work. This is especially true of David Butler's work (Figs. 356–359). Butler makes tin cutouts as if he were a primitive Matisse, and at the same time creates works not unlike the late sculptures of Frank Stella in their use of color and complex placement of shapes.

Butler has said that his work grows out of his dreams, but Bessie Harvey (Figs. 360–363) says hers is born when she looks at a tree, a branch or a stump and it reveals to her the sculpture she is directed to make. If asked what her sculptures are about, she answers that they are about life, which is why Fig. 361 is entitled "The Spirit of Love."

Jessie Aaron, like several other naive artists, avows that he was first inspired by a vision. God, he said, told him to carve but did not tell him what to carve. In his case, his vision did not manifest itself as a religious message or materialize in religious images, but rather served as a key to unlock what was stored in his mind. It may have functioned as a rationalization for the time spent in carving: it is difficult to argue with a command from God.

Aside from the anonymous ones, about whom there is no information, the contemporary artists whose works are reproduced here have had limited educations, they live in economically depressed areas and they did not turn to art until their later years, when their talents emerged more or less completely developed, almost as if their potential had been hidden away in a mental drawer during the early part of their lives. The work and environmentals created by these artists who are outside the norm are generally considered to be junk by the average run of people coming into contact with them. It is only because of the efforts of individuals with an appreciation for the eclecticism of contemporary art movements, who have recognized works like these as, for all their naiveté, part of the contemporary art scene, that any of these works are preserved.

There is little evidence that this type of art existed in the nineteenth century, but if it did, such artists were no doubt considered crazy or their

FIG. 332. *Empire State Building.* Anonymous. Cherry wood. Found in New Jersey. This construction, composed of thousands of hand-cut and -shaped pieces of cherry wood all interlocking without the use of any glue, nails or screws, is said to have been made by a man who worked on the construction of the actual Empire State Building. Ca. 1931. H: 7′ 10″; W: 30″; D: 30″. (Collection of Frank Maresca)

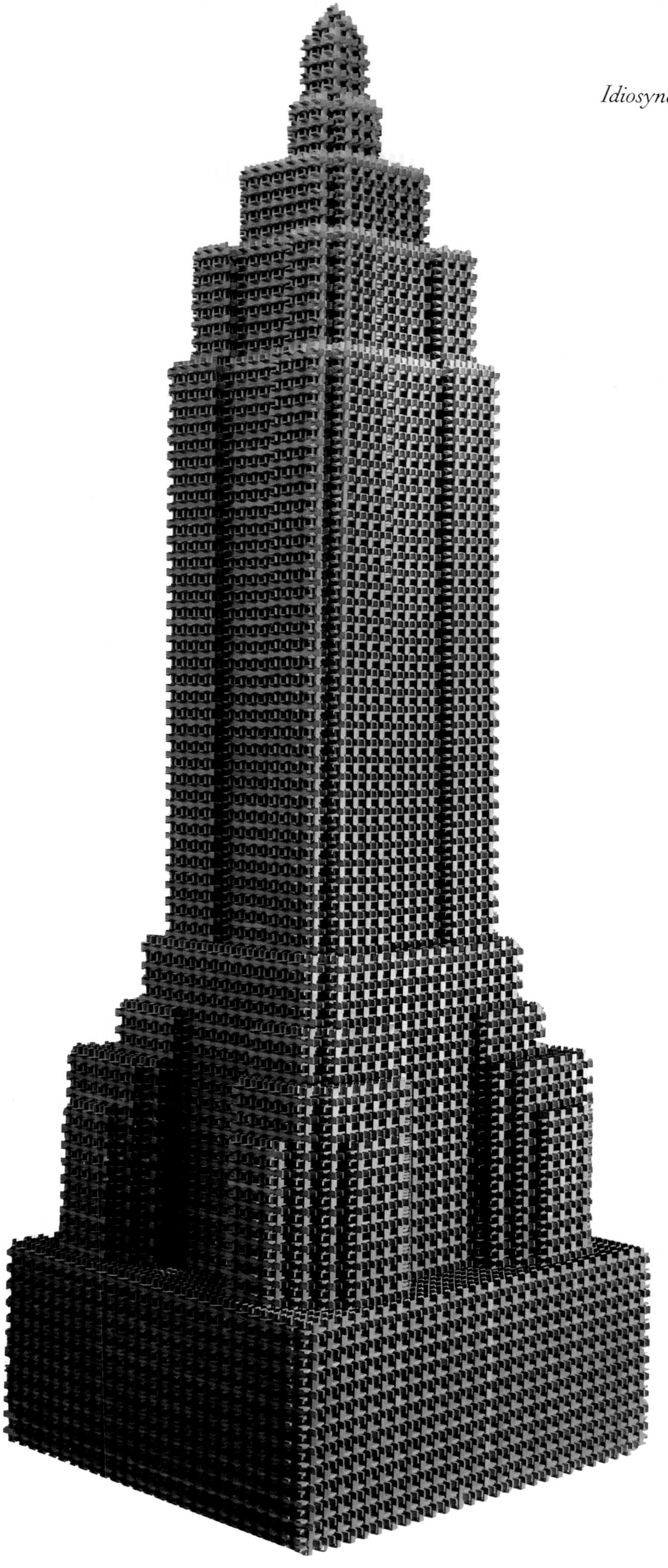

Wire figures. Anonymous.

FIG. 333. (LEFT) H: 8"; L: 11".

FIG. 334. (BELOW) H: 5¹/₂"; W: 3¹/₄".

FIG. 335. (OPPOSITE) H, 12"; W: 3³/₄".

Wire, scraps of colored paper, ribbons. These fetishlike figures, together with well over a hundred similar ones, were found in front of a transient hotel in central Philadelphia. They were strewn about the sidewalk as if they had been tossed out of a window. Nothing more is known about them, but it seems apparent that they were the obsessive fantasms of a reclusive mind. Ca. 1950–70. (Courtesy Janet Fleisher Gallery and Cavin-Morris, Inc.)

work was regarded as outrageous; hence chances of its survival would have been remote. Nonetheless, occasional pieces from the late nineteenth and early twentieth century have surfaced, indicating that there were, even then, artists who marched to a different drummer or whose vision subverted the conventions of the period. The assemblage in Fig. 331 is apparently a kinetic sculpture, but in fact it neither has a use nor is capable of any motion. It was made by a man said to be mentally ill. Yet given the fact that we have come upon the work of several naive—self-taught—artists who are perfectly lucid and mentally healthy but produce art outside the cultural norm, it seems fair to question whether the allegations concerning the mental state of that artist are in fact valid.

The actual or ultimate utility of many of these pieces remains a mystery, as in the example of the anonymous burl head (Fig. 349). It has a distinctly eerie quality, and the artist's purpose in making it is difficult to

surmise since it shows no evidence of having been worn as a mask or hung on a wall, nor is there any way to make it stand on its own.

The art and artists selected for this section are only the tip of the iceberg of what may well be a considerable number of artists having little or no contact with contemporary art. Yet the art they produce, because it is so eclectic, so deviant from the norm (Figs. 358 and 359), is in effect the naive coeval of the trends in modern and contemporary art. Though some of the artists have been discovered, others remain to be found, and still others will never be noticed and their work will simply vanish.

Four works by Moses Ogden.

FIG. 336. (OPPOSITE BELOW) *Figure of animal.* Unknown species. Maple. Ca. 1890–1910. H: 14″; W: 23″; D: 6″. (Collection of Peter Tillou)

FIG. 337. (OPPOSITE) *Head of man.* Maple burl. Ca. 1890–1910. H: 8″; W: 5¹/₄″; D: 5″. (Collection of Peter Tillou)

FIG. 338. (RIGHT) *Figure of woman.* Maple, fiber hair. Ca. 1890–1910. H: 26″; W: 13″; D: 8″. (Collection of Peter Tillou)

FIG. 339. (BELOW) *Head of man.* Maple burl. Ca. 1890–1910. H: 9″; W: 10″; D: 6″. (Collection of Peter Tillou)

MOSES OGDEN was born in the 1840s, and served in the Civil War. He worked as a wagon maker, and carved pieces to exhibit and sell at local fairs. He called himself "The Jackknife Artist." He built a small cabin for himself in Angelica, New York, and filled it inside and out with his carvings. It became known locally as "Moses Ogden's Wonderland."

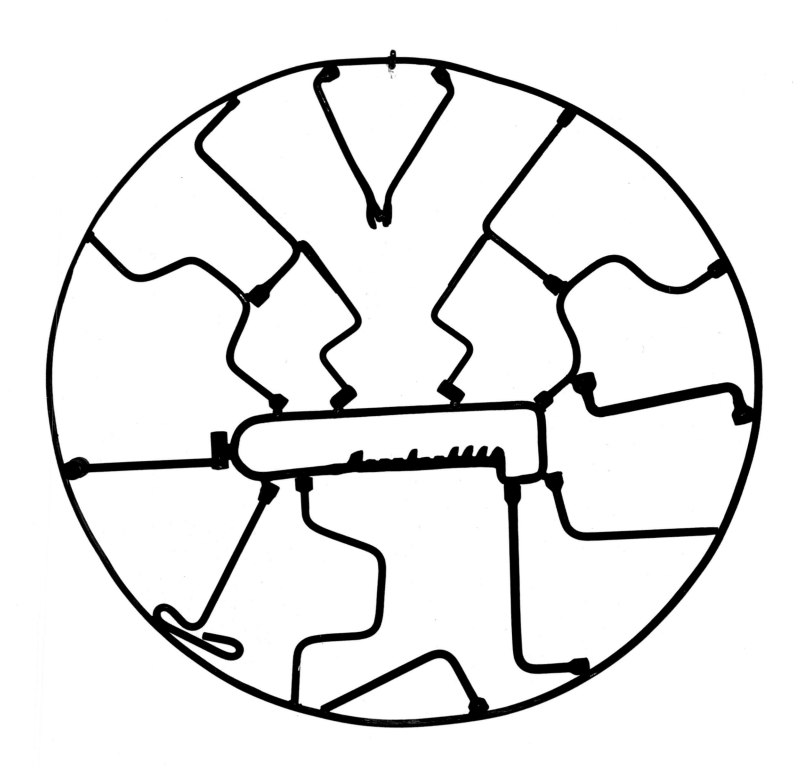

FIGS. 340–343. *Fence of wheels* by Rodney Rosebrook. Welded metal and tools. Rosebrook, now in his eighties, is a retired cowboy and blacksmith living in Redmond, Oregon. For over thirty years he has been collecting old tools and metal objects for what he calls his "Old Time Museum," which is actually an old barn housing thousands of artifacts of the Old West. The wheels shown are part of a metal fence that is strong in composition but lyrical in effect. The fence once bordered the land near his museum. Ca. 1970–75. Diameter: 42". (Private Collection)

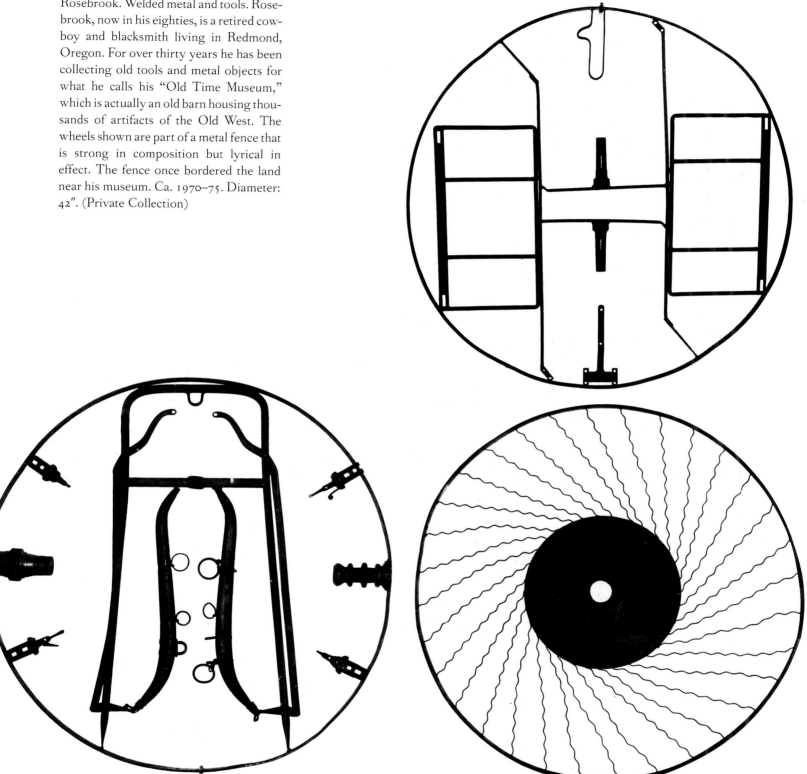

FIG. 344. (LEFT) *Aluminum Pot Cover Face* by Hawkins Bolden. Diameter 10": ca. 1987. (Collection of Frank Maresca)

FIG. 345. (BELOW) *Plastic Chair Seat Face* by Hawkins Bolden. Plastic, canvas fabric. Ca. 1987. H: 27"; W: 15 1/2". (Collection of Roger Ricco)

HAWKINS BOLDEN was born in Tennessee in 1914. Bolden was struck in the head at five years of age by his twin brother, and the blow led to total blindness and epilepsy. He lives now in Montgomery, Alabama, and says that he makes his objects as protection for himself and his surroundings. The objects often suggest faces or are mask-like. They are usually constructed of metal, wood, cloth, and other found materials, and placed on poles stuck in the ground surrounding his home. These pieces are created solely by the sense of touch and a vivid imagination.

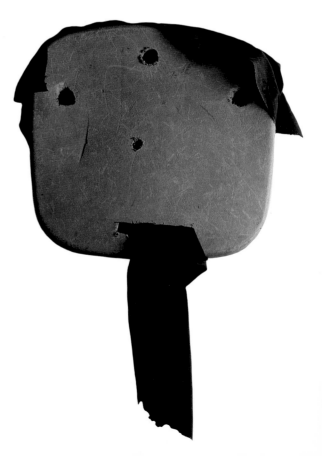

FIG. 346. (RIGHT) *Figure seated on a bench* by Dilmus Hall. H: 13″; W: 10″. (Collection of Roger Ricco)

FIG. 347. (LEFT) *Crucifix* by Dilmus Hall. H: 17″; platform: 16″ × 12″. (Collection of Roger Ricco)

FIG. 348. (OPPOSITE) *Figure* by Dilmus Hall. H: 13½″. (Collection of Roger Ricco)

DILMUS HALL was born March 15, 1900, in Florida and now lives in Georgia. He has worked as a hotel porter, a laborer, and was a soldier in World War I. A religious man, he thinks of himself as a teacher and philosopher, and therein lies the inspiration for his sculptures. As a youngster, he used pitch from trees as modeling material, and the techniques he taught himself then are evident in these works. Wood, plastic wood, metal, beads, paint. 1983–84.

FIG. 349. (OPPOSITE) *Head.* Anonymous. Burl. Found in New York State. The natural burl form has been minimally carved. Late 19th, early 20th century. H: 10″; W: 10″; D: 9″. (Marvel Collection)

FIG. 350. (ABOVE) *Root monster.* Anonymous. Roots, applied cork, paint, glass marble eyes. This phantasmagoric creature, found in Maine, differs from other root sculpture not only in its size but in its feral grotesqueness. 19th century. H: 20″; W: 16″; L: 72″. (Blumert-Fiore Collection)

FIG. 351. (OPPOSITE) *Cypress face* by Jessie Aaron. Cast plastic resin eyes. Ca. 1978–79. H: 29″; W: 28″; D: 3″. (Collection of Chase Manhattan Bank)

FIG. 352. (RIGHT) *Figure with alligator* by Jessie Aaron. Cypress wood with burn marks and gray paint. Ca. 1978. H: 67″. (Collection of Jack and Ali Clift)

JESSIE AARON carved these two figures when he was in his nineties. At that time he had been carving only a few years. The Lord, he said, had come to him in a dream and told him to carve, but "He didn't tell me what to carve." His first carving, done with a pocketknife that very night, was a face in a tree in his yard. His large body of work includes many pieces exhibited in the landmark "Black Folk Art" show presented at the Corcoran Gallery in Washington, D.C., in 1981.

FIG. 353. (RIGHT) *Sandstone receptacle.* Anonymous. Although the various figures may have symbolic meaning and the three holes in the piece indicate it was a receptacle, its actual use and meaning are unknown. Late 19th, early 20th century. H: 5″; W: 6½″; D: 2″. (The Hall Collection of American Folk and Isolate Art)

FIG. 354. (BELOW) *Decorated teapot.* Anonymous. Ceramic teapot, found objects, putty, radiator paint. A hobby craft that became popular around the turn of the century, not only in this country but abroad, was that of covering a jar or vase with putty, embedding in it a variety of small memorabilia and painting over the whole with metallic paint. Late 19th, early 20th century. H: 10½″. (Courtesy Ricco-Maresca Gallery)

FIG. 355. (OPPOSITE) *Child in a high chair.* Anonymous. Found metal and radio parts, electric cord, toys. Found in San Francisco. There is in this assemblage of machinery parts a touch of malevolence, for when it is plugged in, it becomes a child having a tantrum. The child's arms bang the tray, the feet stamp, the tiny light-bulb eyes flash. Its sporadic wails are actually static from a 1930s radio. Also shocked into action are, among other things, madly flickering lights, a mooing toy cow and brushes and springs that rattle and roll. When water is poured into a small funnel behind the child, it wets.

This kinetic sculpture, made to entertain, has elegant antecedents in the ornate automata of earlier eras which were animated by clockworks. It is, as well, something of a precursor of the satirical sculptures of Dadaists like Richard Stankiewicz and Jean Tinguely, who used old machine parts and junk to create figurative sculptures that mocked or criticized industrialism by doing useless, repetitive work. 20th century. H: 46″; W: 2′; D: 2′. (Courtesy William Greenspon)

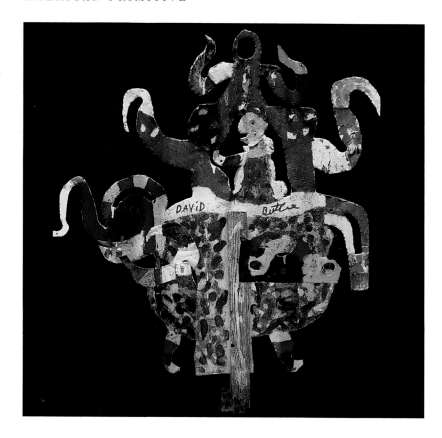

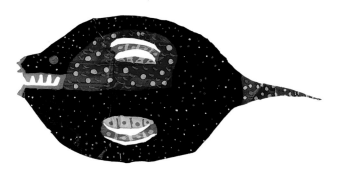

Four works by David Butler.

FIG. 356. (LEFT) *Elephant and rider.* H: 26″; W: 34″. (Collection of Jack and Ali Clift)

FIG. 357. (BELOW LEFT) *"Flag" with two turtles and starfish.* 2′3″ × 3′2″. (Blumert-Fiore Collection)

FIG. 358. (BELOW) *Stingray.* H: 31″; W: 40″. (Collection of Roger Ricco)

FIG. 359. (OPPOSITE) *Man with three legs.* H: 27″; W: 21″. (Collection of Roger Ricco)

DAVID BUTLER, the eldest of eight children and born in St. Mary Parish, Louisiana, now lives in Patterson, Louisiana. As a boy, he enjoyed drawing and whittling whenever a break in his numerous household and family chores permitted him the leisure. As a married adult, however, his jobs as a sawmill laborer left him little time for such pleasures until a work-related accident in his late forties forced him into retirement. It was then that he began his painted and folded metal sculptures. The pieces shown here are chiseled and snipped tin with polychrome.

Butler is religious, but the numerous works that populate his yard are inspired less by devotion than by the fantasies and odd creatures he sees in his dreams. His work has been exhibited at the Museum of Art in New Orleans and in Washington, D.C., at the Corcoran Gallery's "Black Folk Art" show.

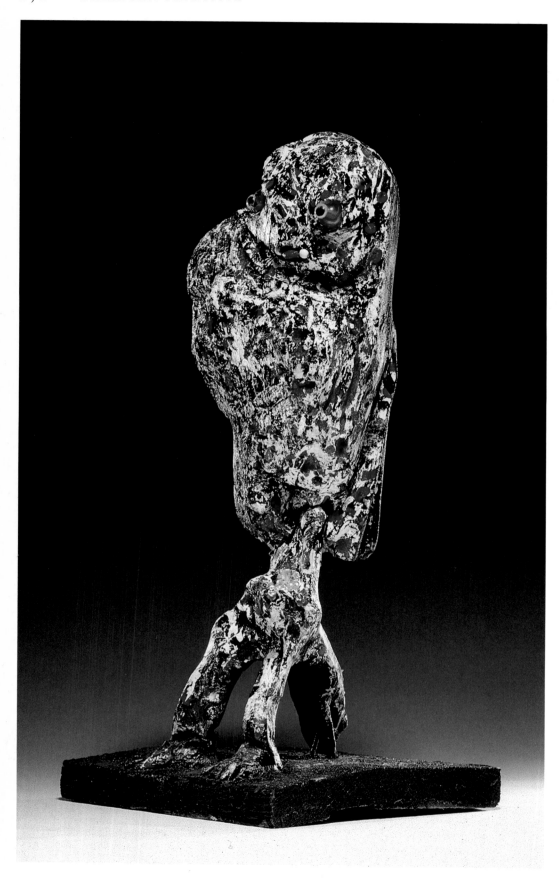

Four works by Bessie Harvey.

FIG. 360. (LEFT) *Owl*. Wood with polychrome. Ca. 1985. H: 11″. (Collection of Frank Maresca)

FIG. 361. (OPPOSITE LEFT) *Figure*. Wood with polychrome, composition, hemp. Titled "The Spirit of Love." Ca. 1985. H, detail: 16″; overall: 25″. (Collection of Edward Shoffstall)

FIG. 362. (OPPOSITE RIGHT) *Birth*. Wood with polychrome, composition, metallic glitter, shells. Ca. 1986. H: 31″; W: 12″; D: 8″. (Collection of Cavin-Morris)

FIG. 363. (OPPOSITE BELOW) *Untitled*. Wood with polychrome, composition, glass eyes, shells. Ca. 1986. H: 27″; W: 27″; D: 16″. (Collection of Cavin-Morris)

BESSIE HARVEY was born October 11, 1928, in Dallas, Georgia, the seventh of thirteen children in a family that was only barely able to survive the most wretched poverty. Harvey married at fourteen and raised eleven children almost single-handedly. She was subject to visions, and said she saw faces, and when most of her children approached adulthood she began to make them "real" by creating "dolls" out of tree roots, cloth, hair, feathers, wood, putty, paint and oddments of jewelry. Though the dolls, she has said, "contain the souls of ancient Africans," they are also an expression of her intense religiosity as well as her strong creative drive.

FIG. 364. (BELOW AND DETAIL RIGHT) *Nutcracker.* Anonymous. Wood, varnish. The carving is evocative of figures carved by the Bena Lulua tribe of Africa. The motion of the handle rocks the baby—a touch of humor in an otherwise dramatic sculpture. 19th century. H: 8½"; L: 11". (Private Collection)

FIG. 365. (OPPOSITE) *Tree of heads.* Anonymous. Wood, tree branches, polychrome, marble eyes, plastic accessories. Ca. 1940–50. H: 67". (Private Collection)

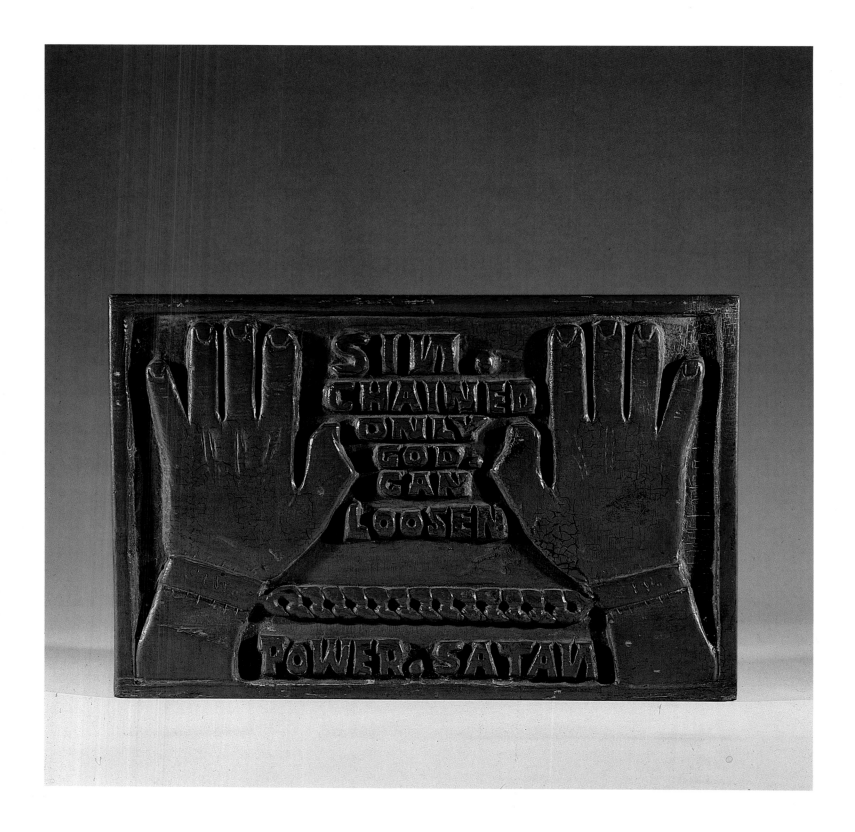

11

RELIGION
and SYMBOLISM

FIG. 366. *Wood plaque.* Anonymous. Poplar with polychrome. A poignant work of prison art from an upstate New York penitentiary. First quarter 20th century. H: 11½"; W: 17½". (Collection of Frank Maresca)

RELIGION AND spiritual ideology have inspired much of the world's art ever since the first human beings formed the concept of deities and sought to objectify them. Sir Herbert Read, in *The Art of Sculpture,* remarks that in the making of cult objects—by which he meant idols, fetishes and totems, but surely the figures of religious organizations should be included—a "close relationship is established between the form and the power of the work of art . . . an object is created in the belief that it will be immediately endowed with mana." Mana, he explains, is a word from anthropology, and is the name "given to that power immanent in all things . . . even inanimate objects . . . the power . . . energizing all magic and ritual."[14]

The importance of art, then, even its necessity in involving the emotions of a constituency and in preserving the faith, has provided stimulation for professional and naive artists in all cultures. The difference between the two groups, however, is that the professional is ordinarily commissioned (i.e., paid) to create a work. The naive, in contrast, is impelled by belief and becomes an artist as a servant of faith.

Thus it was fervor, not artistic ambition, that urged sculptors Josephus Farmer (Figs. 390 and 391), Elijah Pierce (Figs. 376 and 377) and the

Reverend Howard Finster (Figs. 378 and 379), and possibly even Edgar Tolson (Fig. 367), although his religiosity was tempered by alcohol.

Pierce and Farmer shared very similar backgrounds. Both were rural Southerners and grandchildren of slaves; although evidently not known to each other, each used much the same sculptural techniques. Pierce was a barber and Farmer worked at a variety of jobs, but each also preached and considered preaching his true profession. Further, each used his works for the same purpose: to illustrate sermons, Bible stories and historical and contemporary events relevant to the black communities.

Finster, though he, too, had worked at more than one trade, embraced the ministry as his sole profession and did not turn to art until he was fifty, in the late 1960s, when the intense revivalist energy of his sermonizing threatened his health. He asked the Lord what to do, and the answer was: Make art. He began to paint portraits, make assemblage sculpture and build his still unfinished "Garden of Eden" grotto. His works are embellished with his own exhortative versions of the Scriptures, but that is the extent of his preaching. He does not, as Farmer and Pierce did until they were too old, go out into the field, though he will accept most invitations to come and discuss his art work.

Much of Finster's oeuvre (Figs. 378 and 379) is exemplary of art that very likely would only have been made in this century: art composed of the detritus of a society whose economy is based on rapid replacement of consumer goods. He uses junk, industrial and household throwaways: machine and car parts, plumbing, radios, TV sets, bottles, broken mirrors, costume jewelry, toys, buttons, beads, etc. Artists like Finster are what Verna Greenfield calls "recyclers,"[15] those who, like Stanley Papio (Fig. 3), salvage and use discarded materials and turn them into meaningful creations. Many mainstream artists have made use of these free materials as well: Louise Nevelson, Edward Kleinholtz and Marcel Duchamp come to mind. Still, Finster's assemblages and his junk-embedded grotto are, perhaps unintentionally, as much monuments to the profligate wastefulness of our consumer society as they are paeans to his religious beliefs and his escape into the bosom of God.

As in mainstream religious art, the crucifixion and Calvary are frequent themes. Depiction of the Holy Family enthroned is not common, and rare indeed is any depiction, naive or professional, as serenely beautiful as that attributed to John Philip Yaeger (Fig. 382).

FIG. 367. (BELOW) *Snake mantel support* by Edgar Tolson. Pine with polychrome. Tolson (1904–83), a Kentucky descendant of 17th-century English settlers, called himself a wood carver but was also a preacher, farmer, cobbler and chair maker as well as a hard-drinking, tobacco-chewing, storytelling philosopher. This mantelpiece, one of a pair, is one of his earliest carvings with a biblical reference. Ca. 1942. H: 49"; W: 4¹/₂". (The Hall Collection of American Folk and Isolate Art)

Symbolism that represents one's orthodoxy is not intrinsically different from symbolism that is the focus of ritual or represents home and country. Each is concerned with beliefs and idealism, which can be felt with such intensity as to spur either the offer of one's life or the making of a work of art that externalizes one's loyalty in imagery and so gives meaning to one's existence in an increasingly irrational world.

No doubt, then, intense patriotism inspired the two simple, primitively expressive figures representing the Statue of Liberty (Figs. 392 and 393), as well as the watch hutch (Fig. 400), an extraordinarily fine and imaginative tribute to American history and freedom, and the two pie crimpers (Figs. 398 and 399). Uncle Sam is almost as frequent a subject as the Statue of Liberty, and while not often portrayed with reverence, is nonetheless treated with humorous affection (Figs. 394 and p. 4). Lodge rituals often center on fascinatingly enigmatic figures, like Figs. 395 and 396, while repentance without doubt guided the hand that carved the wood plaque Fig. 366.

FIG. 368. (RIGHT) *Ohio sewer-tile head.* Anonymous. Glazed clay. It was not uncommon for tile workers to use clay left over at the end of the day to make personal objects and whimsies. This one is signed "El Diablo" on the back. Late 19th century. H: 9"; W: 4"; D: 3½". (Collection of Frank Maresca)

FIG. 369. (OPPOSITE) *Adam and Eve and the snake* by William Edmondson. Limestone. Edmondson (1865?–1951) was a handyman and stoneworker prior to the day he received a command from God to carve stone. Both Edward Weston and Louise Dahl photographed Edmondson and his sculpture, and through their photography his work came to the attention of the art world. In 1931, the Museum of Modern Art held a one-man show. This piece came to light in time for the 1981 retrospective exhibition of his work at the Tennessee State Museum. H: 22½″; W: 30″; D: 12″. (Private Collection)

FIG. 370. (RIGHT) *Eve in the Garden of Eden.* Anonymous. Maple burl, varnish. Found in New England. A particularly sensuous depiction of Eve. Ca. 1920–30. H: 13″; W: 13″. (Private Collection)

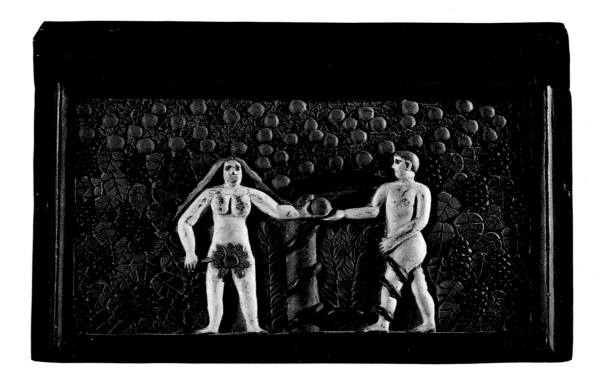

FIG. 371. (ABOVE) *Box with Adam and Eve on the cover.* Anonymous. Pine with polychrome. Found in Evanston, Illinois. Ca. 1880. H: 7 1/4″; W: 11 1/2″; D: 2 1/2″. (Collection of Harvey and Rosalyn Pranian)

FIG. 372. (LEFT) *Eve in the Garden of Eden.* Anonymous. Pine. Origin unknown. Early 20th century. H: 8″; W: 6″. (Private Collection)

FIG. 373. (ABOVE) *Marble plaque* by Popeye Reed. This low-relief biblical carving is
one of the few pieces that Popeye Reed,
from Jackson, Ohio, created in marble. A
prolific artist, he worked primarily in sandstone and wood. Ca. 1960–70. H: 10″;
W: 10″; D: 1¼″. (Collection of Jeff Way)

FIG. 374. (ABOVE RIGHT) *Brick with angel
motif.* Anonymous. Clay. Found in Pennsylvania and believed to be from a church
or chapel. 18th century. H: 5″; W: 5″. (Collection of Charles and Alexandra Van
Horne)

FIG. 375. (RIGHT) *Sandstone capital.* Anonymous. Probably New England. The face
of the angel is repeated with slight varia-
tions on each side of this sculpted capital.
Late 18th century. 9½″ square. (Private
Collection)

FIG. 376. (ABOVE) *Christ with sheep plaque* by Elijah Pierce. Wood with polychrome. Ca. 1960–70. H: 12″; W: 12″. (Private Collection)

FIG. 377. (OPPOSITE) *Crucifixion scene* by Elijah Pierce. Wood with polychrome, glitter, toy trees. Ca. 1970. H: 19″; W: 18″; D: 15″. (Collection of Geoffrey Holder)

ELIJAH PIERCE (1892–1983) was, in addition to being a barber, a sometime itinerant preacher. Like Josephus Farmer, he used his carvings, which he sold, as adjuncts to his preaching.

I WAS SENT TO THIS PLANET AS NOAH BEFORE THE FLOOD I AM TO REACH THE WHOLE WORLD WITH FACTS ABOUT GOD AND JESUS ABOUT LIFE AND DEATH HEAVEN AND HELL. MY WHOLE LIFE IS TO BE DEDICATED TO SOULS OF EARTH PLANET I HAVE SACRIFICED ALL SPORTS NEW CARS, AND HOMES TO HONOR MY MISSION FROM GOD.

HE THAT BELIEVETH AND IS BAPTISED SHALL BE SAVED DONT PUT IT OFF

JESUS SAVES

JESUS WILL COMEBACK FOR HIS PEOPLE

HEAVEN IS MY NEXT MOVE

THE GREATEST RICHES IS TO GET TO HEAVEN

I LOVE MY CALLING

Two works by the Reverend Howard Finster.

FIG. 378. (OPPOSITE) *Box.* Wood, mirrors, tin, painted beads, found objects, Plexiglas. 1983. H: 28″; W: 19″; D: 3 1/2″. (Private Collection)

FIG. 379. (BELOW) *Assemblage from "The Garden of Eden."* H: 14″; W: 13″. (Collection of Roger Ricco)

HOWARD FINSTER (b. 1917) became a sculptor, painter and builder of "environments" in the late 1960s. When not working on his "Garden of Eden" and four-story "World's Folk Art Church" built of cement and found materials, he paints and devises portable assemblages with religious exhortations as their themes.

FIG. 380. (RIGHT) *Tramp art shrine.* Anonymous. Wood, polychrome, glass mirror, lightweight textured cardboard. Found in western Pennsylvania. Ca. 1880–1900. H: 43½"; W: 26"; D: 17". (Rochester Memorial Art Museum)

FIG. 381. (BELOW) *Adoration of the Christ Child: "Gloria in Excelsis Deo."* Anonymous. Wood with polychrome, metal, bell. Early 20th century. H: 22"; W: 15"; D: 9½". (Herbert Waide Hemphill, Jr., Collection)

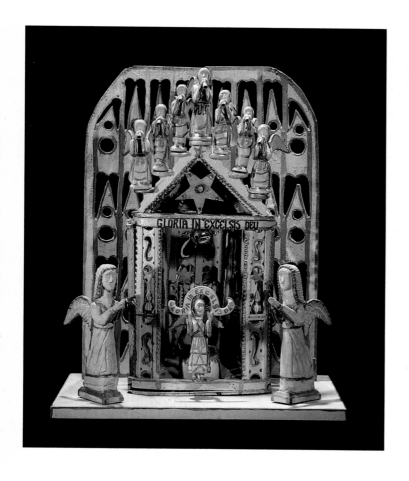

FIG. 382. (OPPOSITE) *Holy Family.* Attributed to John Philip Yaeger, Baltimore, Maryland. Poplar, pine, maple, varnish. This piece, found in Baltimore, shows a strong Germanic influence. Yaeger, who died in 1899, once studied for the priesthood, and was a carver by trade. All three figures bear the marks of the stigmata on hands and feet. Ca. 1870–90. H: 33"; W: 28"; D: 19". (Private Collection)

FIG. 383. (ABOVE) *Resurrection scene.* Anonymous. Wood, traces of paint. This tableau was one of many New Testament scenes that adorned the porch of a private home in Iowa. Ca. 1915. H, tallest figure: 11⁷⁄₈″; base: 14³⁄₄″ × 5¹⁄₂″. (Private Collection)

FIG. 384. (LEFT) *Crucifixion* by Jim Colclough. Redwood, linseed oil. Colclough, born in 1901 in California, began carving around 1965, after his wife died. Ca. 1965–75. H: 51″; W, armspread: 38″. (Herbert Waide Hemphill, Jr., Collection)

FIG. 385. (ABOVE) *Crucifixion.* Anonymous. Pine with paint. Found in Washington State and thought to have been made by a Yakima Indian. Early 20th century. H, center figure: 12¹/₂″; H, side figures: 11¹/₂″. (Collection of William Greenspon)

FIG. 386. (RIGHT) *Crucifixion.* Anonymous. Wood with polychrome. This piece, found in Vermont, has its original paint. Familiar symbols of death and resurrection, such as the cock, bell, ladder, pole and skull, are applied. Late 19th century. H: 27″; w, at crossbar: 16″. (Brian Collection)

FIG. 387. (LEFT) *Bust of a man with crossed arms.* Wood with polychrome. This figure, probably a teaching aid, was likely made by the Millerites—followers of William Miller (1782–1849), who believed the world would come to an end in 1844. The carving is in sections, each having numerous small vertical holes, possibly to hold rolled disks of paper on which were written biblical verses. 19th century. H: 14″. (Collection of Harvey and Rosalyn Pranian)

FIG. 388. (OPPOSITE) *Child and celestial sphere.* Wood with polychrome. Found in Montana, possibly a Christ child figure from a fraternal lodge. Ca. 1900–20. H: 25″. (Brian Collection)

FIG. 389. (BELOW) *"Diabolus Panel,"* Anonymous. Pine with cypress back, polychrome. Found in New Orleans. Research indicates that this panel was made by a regional cult or group probably of Afro-American origin. The plaque depicts the Devil and his consort, and surrounding scenes appear to show the Devil's assistants escorting humans to the lower levels of Hell. The bodies of the entwined snakes in the upper panels depict the triple sixes, an occult symbol associated with Devil worship. All of these scenes and symbols take place within a carved brickwork motif, and very likely indicate the above-ground crypts that were prominently used in New Orleans cemeteries. Early 20th century. L: 48″; H: 18″; D: 2½″. (Marvel Collection)

Two works by Josephus Farmer.

FIG. 390. (OPPOSITE ABOVE) *The Revelation of Prophecy, Matt. 5, Chap. 1.* Ca. 1970–75. H: 30″; W: 50″. (Collection of Mr. and Mrs. Clune Walsh)

FIG. 391. (OPPOSITE BELOW) *The Seven Wonders of the Ancient World.* Ca. 1970–75. H: 30″; W: 50″. (Herbert Waide Hemphill, Jr., Collection)

JOSEPHUS FARMER, the grandson of a slave, was born in Tennessee in 1894 and migrated to Illinois in 1917. In 1922, deeply affected by a church service, he embraced the Pentecostal faith and became a street preacher and church founder. The pieces shown here are redwood and enamel house paint. In Farmer's own words, his carving is "just a gift, a gift from God." (From a detailed study of Farmer and his work in *The Gift of Josephus Farmer,* by Joanna Cubbs, University of Wisconsin, Milwaukee Art History Gallery, November 1982.)

FIG. 394. (OPPOSITE) *Uncle Sam*. Anonymous. Sheet metal (tin). Uncle Sam, long a favorite subject of self-taught sculptors, here holds a flag and a book. He may have been made by a tinsmith as a demonstration of his skill. Late 19th, early 20th century. H: 29". (Private Collection)

FIG. 392. (ABOVE) *The Statue of Liberty.* Anonymous. Wood, composition, with gold paint. Hollow construction. Mid-20th century. H: 41". (Private Collection)

FIG. 393. (RIGHT) *The Statue of Liberty.* Anonymous. Pine, varnish. Southern origin. Ca. 1920–30. H: 20½". (Private Collection)

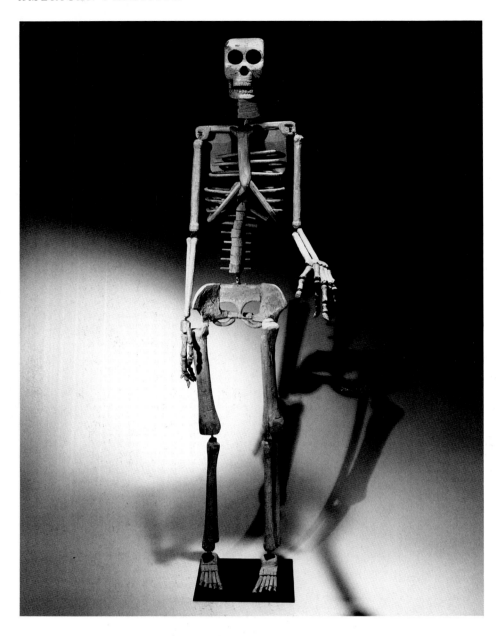

FIG. 395. (LEFT) *Skeleton.* Anonymous. Pine with polychrome. This 19th-century handmade skeleton was found in Vermont. Probably a lodge figure. H: 68½″. (Courtesy William Greenspon)

FIG. 396. (BELOW) *Egyptian figure.* Anonymous. Wood with gold paint. Found in Jackson, Michigan. Once used in a fraternal lodge. The two hinged doors in the chest open to reveal a compartment with drawers in which ceremonial material was probably kept. The outstretched hands also served as candle holders. Ca. 1920–30. H: 38″; W: 19″; D: 20″. (Collection of Lisa Stone and Don Howlett)

FIG. 397. (OPPOSITE) *Carved box.* Anonymous. Wood, stained and varnished. The lodge symbols of hand and heart and the three chain links suggest this box was used in a fraternal lodge, possibly one connected with the shoemaking trade. Ca. 1900–20. H: 21″; W: 13″. (Brian Collection)

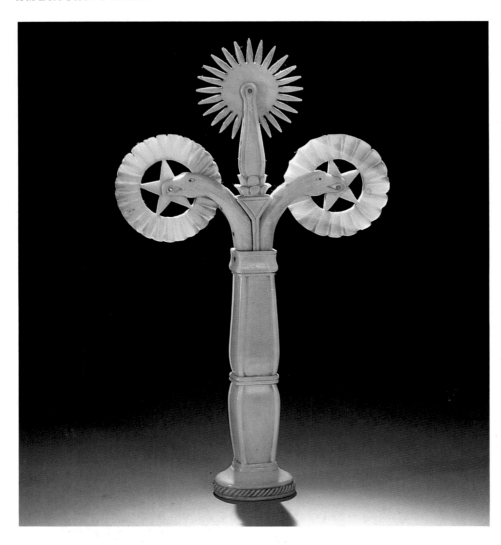

FIG. 398. (LEFT) *Scrimshaw pie crimper with sun, stars and eagles.* Anonymous. Whale ivory. 19th century. L: 8³/₈″; W, across wheels: 4″. (Collection of Howard and Catherine Feldman)

FIG. 399. (BELOW) *Pie crimper and fork.* Anonymous. Whale ivory. An unusual combination of symbols. 19th century. L: 7³/₄″. (Collection of Howard and Catherine Feldman)

FIG. 400. (OPPOSITE) *Watch hutch.* Anonymous. Ivory, varnished mahogany. This elaborate tower has numerous symbols relating to freedom: an eagle and stars, a female figure holding a pole and cap representing the young republic, and a total of eighteen busts, possibly intended to symbolize statesmen. The watch is housed in the top of the tower. Ca. 1900. H: 35″; W: 17″; D: 10″. (Private Collection)

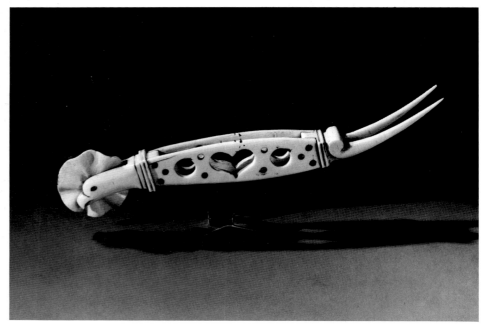

FIG. 401. (LEFT) *Indian attacking a bear.* Anonymous. Pine with polychrome, feathers. Found in Massachusetts. It has been suggested that this small sculpture was copied from a 19th-century magazine, such as the *Police Gazette* or *Harper's*, or from a Beadle dime novel, which had stories and woodcuts of brave Indian scouts. Late 19th century. H: 16″; W: 14″. (Collection of Norman Brosterman)

FIG. 402. (BELOW LEFT) *Political whimsy.* Anonymous. Wood with polychrome. Although carved out of one piece of wood, the figure and the ball move independently from the base. Late 19th, early 20th century. H: 21½″. (Private Collection)

FIG. 403. (OPPOSITE) *Hand holding a chisel.* Anonymous. Wrought iron with hollow shaft. Made to be carried aloft on a pole, probably for ceremonial use in a stonemason's fraternal lodge. Mid- to late 19th century. H: 13½″; W: 9½″; D: 2½″. (Collection of Gary and Cheryl Heimbuch)

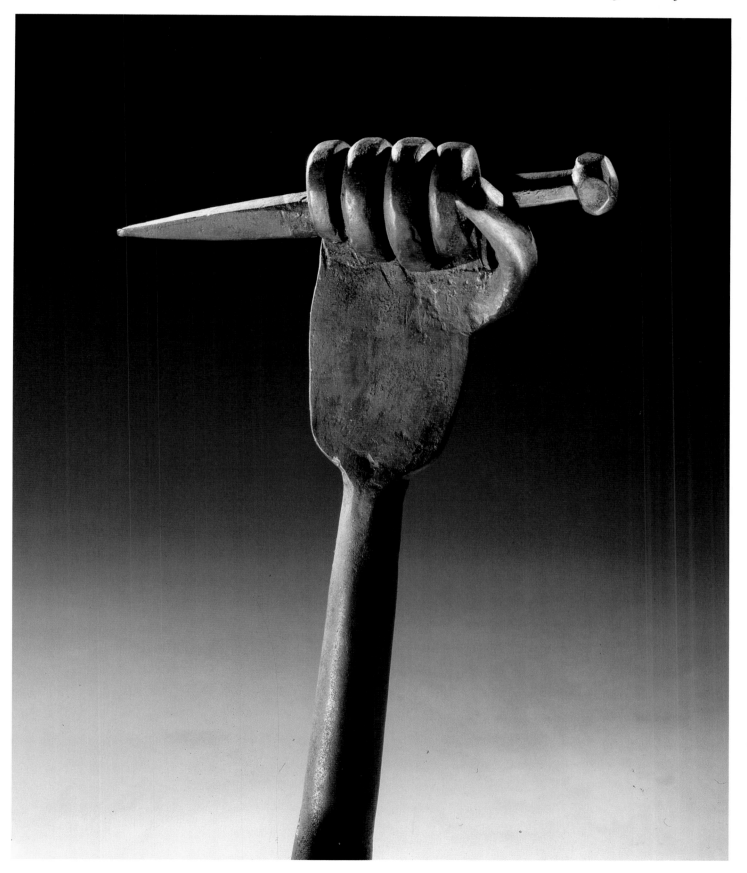

Notes

1. Wayne Craven, *Sculpture in America*, rev. ed. (New York: Cornwall Books, 1984), introduction.

2. John Manfredi, *The Social Limits of Art* (Amherst: University of Massachusetts Press, 1982), introduction, p. 13.

3. Robert Goldwater, *Primitivism in Modern Art*, rev. ed. (New York: Vintage Books, 1968).

4. Eugene W. Metcalf, Jr., "The Problem of American Folk Art," *Maine Antiques Digest,* April 1986.

5. Goldwater, op. cit.

6. Michael Hall, *American Folk Sculpture: The Personal and the Eccentric* (Bloomfield Hills, Mich.: Cranbrook Academy, 1971).

7. Daniel Robbins, "Folk Sculpture Without Folk," in *Folk Sculpture, USA,* ed. Herbert Waide Hemphill, Jr. (Brooklyn, N.Y.: Brooklyn Museum, 1976), pp. 14, 20, 21.

8. Lynette I. Rhodes, *American Folk Art: From the Traditional to the Naive* (Cleveland: Cleveland Museum of Art, 1978), p. 13.

9. Ibid.

10. Erwin Panofsky, *Meaning in the Visual Arts* (Woodstock, N.Y.: Overlook Press, 1974), p. 10.

11. Al Griffin, *"Step Right Up, Folks!"* (Chicago: Henry Regnery Company, 1974), introduction.

12. Arthur H. Lewis, *Carnival!* (New York: Trident Press, 1970), p. 116.

13. Joanna Cubbs, *The Gift of Josephus Farmer* (Milwaukee: University of Wisconsin Press, 1982), p. 7.

14. Herbert Read, *The Art of Sculpture* (Princeton, N.J.: Bollingen Series: A. W. Mellon Lectures in the Fine Arts, Vol. III, Princeton University Press, 1969), p. 42.

15. Verna Greenfield, "Silk Purses from Sows' Ears: An Aesthetic Approach to Recycling," in *Personal Places: Perspectives on Informal Art Environs,* ed. Daniel Franklin Ward (Bowling Green, Ohio: Bowling Green State University Popular Press, 1985).

Bibliography

BOOKS

Ames, Kenneth L. *Beyond Necessity: Art in the Folk Tradition.* Winterthur, Del.: Henry Francis du Pont Winterthur Museum, 1977.

Bazin, Germain. *A Concise History of World Sculpture.* New York: Alpine Fine Arts Collection, Ltd., 1981.

Bishop, Robert. *American Folk Sculpture.* New York: E. P. Dutton & Co., 1974.

———— and Patricia Coblentz. *American Weathervanes and Whirligigs.* New York: E. P. Dutton & Co., 1981.

Boothroyd, A. E. *Fascinating Walking Sticks.* New York and London: White Lion Publishers, 1973.

Cahill, Holger, and Alfred H. Barr, Jr. *Art in America in Modern Times.* New York: Museum of Modern Art in arrangement with Harcourt, Brace and World, 1969.

Chase, Judith Wragg. *Afro-American Art and Craft.* New York: Van Nostrand Reinhold Co., 1971.

Christensen, Erwin O. *Early American Wood Carving.* New York: World Publishing Co., 1952.

————. *American Crafts and Folk Arts.* Washington, D.C.: Robert E. Luce, 1964.

Dike, Catherine. *Cane Curiosa.* Paris: Les Editions de l'Auteur, 1983.

Earnest, Adele. *The Art of the Decoy.* Rev. ed. Exton, Pa.: Schiffer Publishing Co., 1982.

Fitzgerald, Ken. *Weathervanes and Whirligigs.* New York: Brahmhill House, 1967.

Goldwater, Robert. *Primitivism in Modern Art.* Rev. ed. New York: Vintage Books, 1968.

Goodrich, Lloyd. *Three Centuries of American Art.* New York: Frederick A. Praeger, for the Whitney Museum of Art, 1966.

Gottschalk, D. W. *Art and the Social Order.* Chicago: University of Chicago Press, 1951.

Griffin, Al. *"Step Right Up, Folks!"* Chicago: Henry Regnery Co., 1974.

Hemphill, Herbert W., Jr., and Julia Weissman. *Twentieth Century American Folk Art and Artists.* New York: E. P. Dutton & Co., 1974.

Hiller, Mary. *Automata and Mechanical Toys.* London: Jupiter Books, 1976.

Jung, Carl G., ed. *Man and His Symbols.* Garden City, N.Y.: Doubleday & Co., 1964.

Lévi-Strauss, Claude. *The Savage Mind.* Chicago: University of Chicago Press, 1966.

Lewis, Arthur H. *Carnival!* New York: Trident Press, 1970.

Lipman, Jean. *Provocative Parallels.* New York: E. P. Dutton & Co., 1975.

———. *American Folk Art in Wood, Metal and Stone.* New York: Dover Publications, reprint, 1984.

Mackey, William F., Jr. *American Bird Decoys.* Exton, Pa.: Schiffer Publishing Co., 1965.

Manfredi, John. *The Social Limits of Art.* Amherst: University of Massachusetts Press, 1982.

McKendrick, Blake. *Folk Art: Primitive and Naïve in Canada.* Toronto: Methuen, 1983.

Panofsky, Erwin. *Meaning in the Visual Arts.* Woodstock, N.Y.: Overlook Press, 1974.

Paskman, Dailey. *"Gentlemen, Be Seated!"* New York: Clarkson N. Potter, 1976.

Pontus Hulton, K. G. *The Machine as Seen at the End of the Mechanical Age.* New York: Museum of Modern Art, 1968.

Read, Herbert E. *The Art of Sculpture.* Princeton, N.J.: Bollingen Series, A. W. Mellon Lectures in the Fine Arts, Vol. III, Princeton University Press, 1969.

Rose, Barbara. *American Art Since 1900.* New York: Frederick A. Praeger, reprint, 1975.

Rubin, Cynthia Elyce. *Southern Folk Art.* Birmingham, Ala.: Oxmoor House, 1985.

Stein, Kurt. *Canes and Walking Sticks.* York, Pa.: Liberty Cap Books, George Shumway Publisher, 1974.

Steinfelt, Cecilia. *Texas Folk Art.* San Antonio: Texas Monthly Press, 1981.

Vlach, John Michael. *The Afro-American Tradition in the Decorative Arts.* Cleveland: Cleveland Museum of Art, 1978.

Ward, Daniel Franklin, ed. *Personal Places: Perspectives on Informal Art Environs.* Bowling Green, Ohio: Bowling Green State University Popular Press, 1985.

Willet, Frank. *African Art.* New York: Frederick A. Praeger, 1971.

Wingert, Paul S. *Primitive Art: Its Traditions and Styles.* New York: Oxford University Press, 1962.

CATALOGUES

Armstrong, Tom, et al. *Two Hundred Years of American Sculpture.* New York: David R. Godine, in association with the Whitney Museum of American Art, 1976.

Assael, Alyce. *Singular Visions.* East Hampton, N.Y.: Guild Hall Museum, 1985.

Barrett, Didi. *Muffled Voices.* New York: Museum of American Folk Art, May–September, 1986.

Brill, Marna B. *Wood Sculpture of New York State.* New York: Museum of American Folk Art, April 1975.

Cannon, Hal, ed. *Utah Folk Art.* Provo: Brigham Young University Press, with the Utah Arts Council and the Utah Endowment for the Humanities, n.d.

Clisby, Robert D., and Albert Stewart. *Contemporary American Wood Sculpture.* Sacramento: Crocker Art Museum, 1985.

Cubbs, Joanna. *The Gift of Josephus Farmer.* Milwaukee: University of Wisconsin, Milwaukee Art History Gallery, November 1982.

Doty, Robert. *American Folk Art in Ohio Collections.* Akron: Akron Art Institute, and New York: Dodd, Mead, 1976.

Hall, Michael. *American Folk Sculpture: The Personal and the Eccentric.* Bloomfield Hills, Mich.: Cranbrook Academy Art Galleries, November 1971.

Hemphill, Herbert W., Jr., ed. *Folk Sculpture, USA.* Brooklyn: Brooklyn Museum, 1976.

Jones, Louis C. *Outward Signs of Inner Beliefs: Symbols of American Patriotism.* Cooperstown, N.Y.: New York State Historical Association, 1975.

Larsen-Martin, Susan, and Lauri Robert Martin. *Pioneers in Paradise: Folk and Outsider Artists on the West Coast.* Long Beach, Calif.: Long Beach Museum of Art, 1985.

List, Clair. *Narrative Wood.* Washington, D.C.: Corcoran Gallery of Art, 1981.

Livingston, Jane, and John Beardsley. *Black Folk Art in America, 1930–80.* Washington, D.C.: Corcoran Gallery of Art, 1982.

Mainardi, Patricia. *American Sculpture: Folk and Modern.* Flushing, N.Y.: Queens Museum, 1977.

Rhodes, Lynette I. *American Folk Art: From the Traditional to the Naive.* Cleveland: Cleveland Museum of Art, 1978.

Stewart, Albert. *Contemporary American Wood Sculpture.* Sacramento: Crocker Art Museum, 1984.

Vogue, Susan, and Francis N'Diaye. *Masterpieces from the Musée de l'Homme.* New York: Center for African Art and Harry N. Abrams, 1985.

Wadsworth, Anna, et al. *Missing Pieces: Georgia Folk Art, 1770–1976.* Atlanta: Georgia Council for the Arts and Humanities, 1976.

Waingrow, Jeff. *American Wildfowl Decoys.* New York: E. P. Dutton & Co., in association with the Museum of American Folk Art, 1985.

ARTICLES

Bishop, Robert. "America's Windborne Art." *Portfolio,* April–May 1979.

Gordon, Leah. "Vanes of the Wind." *Smithsonian Magazine,* 1971.

Greenfield, Verna. "Silk Purses from Sows' Ears: An Aesthetic Approach to Recycling." In *Personal Places,* ed. Daniel Franklin Ward. Bowling Green, Ohio: Bowling Green State University Popular Press, 1985.

Hall, Michael. "The Problem of Martin Ramirez: Folk Art Criticism as Cosmologies of Coercion." In *The Clarion,* vol. 1, no. 1, Museum of American Folk Art, 1986.

Metcalf, Eugene W., Jr. "The Problem of American Folk Art." *Maine Antiques Digest,* April 1986.

Robbins, Daniel. "Folk Sculpture Without Folk." In *Folk Sculpture, USA,* Brooklyn Museum catalogue.

A NOTE ON THE TYPE

This book was set in Fournier, a type face named for Pierre Simon Fournier, a celebrated type designer in eighteenth-century France. Fournier's type is considered transitional in that it drew its inspiration from the old style yet was ingeniously innovational. After his death in 1768, Fournier was remembered primarily as the author of a famous manual of typography and as a pioneer of the point system. His reputation was enhanced in 1925, when the Monotype Corporation of London revived Fournier's roman and italic.

Composed by The Sarabande Press, New York, New York. Printed and bound by Amilcare Pizzi, S.P.A., Milan, Italy.

Designed by Peter A. Andersen